12

NEW ANGLES
ON
SALMON FISHING

NEW ANGLES ON SALMON FISHING

Captain

PHILIP P. M. GREEN RN ret'd

Illustrated by Michael Loates

London
GEORGE ALLEN & UNWIN
Boston   Sydney

George Allen & Unwin (Publishers) Ltd,
40 Museum Street, London WC1A 1LU, UK

George Allen & Unwin (Publishers) Ltd,
Park Lane, Hemel Hempstead, Herts HP2 4TE, UK

Allen & Unwin Inc.,
9 Winchester Terrace, Winchester, Mass 01890, USA

George Allen & Unwin Australia Pty Ltd,
8 Napier Street, North Sydney, NSW 2060, Australia

First published in 1984

British Library Cataloguing in Publication Data
Green, Philip P. M.
 New angles on salmon fishing.
 1. Salmon fishing
 I. Title
 799.1'755   SH685
 ISBN 0-04-799020-1

Set in 10 on 12 point Palatino by
D. P. Media Limited, Hitchin, Hertfordshire
and printed in Great Britain by
Biddles Ltd, Guildford, Surrey

CONTENTS

TO MY WIFE
for her patient acceptance of grass-widowhood
season after season

ACKNOWLEDGEMENTS

Many people have helped, directly or indirectly, with my fishing education and consequently in the creation of this book. I shall not attempt to list them all because, after fifty years, there are so many that it would be difficult to know where to draw the line. Who could assess the relative importance of one source against another, when sometimes his education has been consciously advanced and sometimes unconsciously?

Certainly I could never have gained any worthwhile knowledge had I not been given a great deal of fishing, and for that I must record my especial gratitude to Colonel W. G. McHardy CVO, MBE, MC, of Woodend, Colonel J. W. Nicol DSO, DL, of Ballogie, J. C. P. Cessford, Captain Roddie Casement OBE, Royal Navy, the late Peter Morris, the late George Paterson, V. W. Huntington of Bonawe, the late Alistair MacLagan, Lt-Colonel Robert Bradford, David Barr and Jack Bridger.

My gratitude also goes out to two friends who have worked so hard on the typed manuscript, Ronald Turner and Miss Hilda Gilbert.

Finally, some of my ideas were first published in *The Field*, *Trout and Salmon* and the magazine of the Salmon and Trout Association. They have been reproduced in this book by courtesy of the respective editors. My thanks to them.

PHILIP GREEN

AUTHOR'S FOREWORD

Do ye ken how to fish for saumon?
   Come awa' an' I'll tell ye;
Dinna trust tae books an' their gammon
   They just try tae *sell* ye;
Leave professors tae read their ain cackle
   An' fish their ain style;
Come awa', Sir, we'll oot wi' *oor* tackle
   An' be busy the while!

That verse summarises exactly what I feel about most books on salmon fishing. I hope that this one will be found interesting enough to justify its existence.

P.G.

1

Experience – The Inherent Pitfalls

Variations in the quality of salmon fishing experience are almost infinite. At one extreme stands the fisherman, often a ghillie, who has spent his whole life on one river, even on one stretch of it. His experience gives him a knowledge of his water which could hardly be rivalled, and it would be very unwise to disregard his advice about how it should be fished.

It is also unwise to assume that such a man will necessarily have a profound knowledge of salmon fishing in general, unless he happens to possess an especially active and inquiring mind. Secure in the success his experience of his water brings him, he will seldom bother himself with the more intractable problems of fish behaviour. As a rule he will just go along with commonly held beliefs and be the natural repository and perpetuator of folklore, especially if he is a ghillie. This is not intended to denigrate his very special value but merely to put it in its proper perspective.

At the other extreme is the man who fishes intensively but who spends a fortnight here or a fortnight there, like a bird hopping from twig to twig. He may become very experienced but may derive less advantage from it than might be supposed. He will get the benefit of much local opinion and advice, certainly, but much of that can be just prejudice and have no value. Alternatively he may find that what he is told on one river conflicts with or completely contradicts what he is told on another. Only if he is particularly intelligent and thoughtful will he be able to sort out the grain from the chaff and so avoid much confusion of mind.

In looking for variety to widen his knowledge he may in any case be setting himself too hard a task. Consider all the different characteristics salmon rivers can possess, each possibly influencing technique or modifying fish behaviour. Rivers can be wide or narrow, long or short. Their water can be acid, alkaline or neutral, normally clear or normally turbid, fast-flowing or sluggish. They can be deep or shallow, turbulent or placid. Their beds can be weedy, rocky, shingly, gravelly, sandy or muddy. They can be mountain rivers or pastoral ones and their banks can be wooded or bare. Their water levels can have a natural rise and fall which is either quick or slow. Alternatively, levels may be influenced by hydroelectric requirements. They can be fed by glacier, loch, bog or aquifer and their orientation and geographical location can differ widely.

Then again they may be mainly spring or mainly autumn rivers, or those which are blessed with spring, autumn and summer runs.

A permutation of all these characteristics would produce so many different types of river that it would need many lifetimes just to fish them all, let alone enough for the resulting knowledge to be worthwhile. The effort would hardly be merited if it did not lead to a better understanding of salmon, which after all are the central figures in the sport.

Historically, experience has not been very helpful in doing that. Numbers of experienced salmon fishermen have given us the benefit of their deductions about fish behaviour over the years, but few of these have proved to be of much value. The parrot-cry 'You never can tell with salmon' does not arise without good reason.

It is easy to see why this has been so. The validity of conclusions about cause and effect cannot be established without there being

16

controls against which the value of related observations can be assessed, and of course it is impracticable to have them when fishing a salmon river. Without them, what is observed may be merely a coincidence or a random happening. It is insufficient to argue that something must be fact because it has been observed often enough (a common misconception). The effect repeatedly observed may not have been properly attributable to the supposed cause, but to an entirely different one which had escaped notice or consideration. If that were otherwise our knowledge of salmon would have advanced further than it has.

The trout fisherman (and many salmon fishermen still let trout fishing influence their thinking) may argue that he has never had any difficulty in making perfectly sound and accurate assessments about when trout will take, and what fly is likely to induce them to do so, without ever having felt the need for controls to guide him, but his situation is an entirely different one. He is dealing with feeding fish whose habits in that respect are already established facts. Indeed, scientists often use the feeding pattern to gauge when fishes are being subjected to stress, and to what extent. This handy yardstick cannot be used for salmon, once they have left the sea. Consequently it is necessary to approach the evaluation of cause and effect quite differently with salmon.

If much of what we have come to believe as fact is not really fact at all, but merely opinion, we need to be very wary of it. Opinion is not necessarily untrustworthy but it tends to become so when fishermen will only believe what they want to believe, or what they have heard stated again and again by others. As Cervantes put it, 'Plenty of people expect to find bacon where there is not so much as a peg to hang it from.'

The salmon fisher does have *some* pegs, if he will only look for them. These are the relevant environmental and physiological ones, as briefly described in the following six chapters. They may not provide him with many answers, but they are basic, and together form a reliable background against which some cherished theories and practices can usefully be viewed.

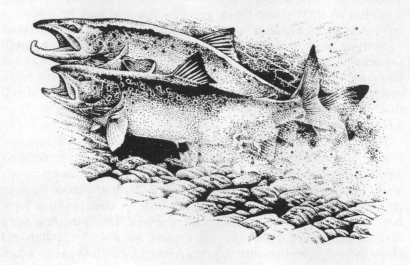

2

The Salmon's Life Cycle

Salmon may return to their native rivers at any time, and anglers usually class them as spring, summer or autumn fish to correspond with the time of year in which the main runs occur. All these classes, together, spawn within a period which normally extends from mid-October to the end of December, although some fish may spawn as late as the following March.

Since scale reading was developed as an exact science in 1904, biologists have discovered that the period spent in the sea by individual fish before returning can vary considerably, and have further classified them as 1 +, 2 +, 3 +, or 4 + fish, depending on the number of winters they have spent there.

This variation in sea life is one of nature's ways of spreading the risk to the species and also partly accounts for the very wide variation in size to be observed between one fish and another. Other than grilse (1 + fish) all are consequently described for convenience as small, large or very large, according to their weight. The criteria for this differ from river to river.

Most of the fish in a run are maiden fish, because the death rate among salmon after spawning, especially among males, is very high. The few which have made the journey before are known as SM fish (SM = spawning mark).

While spawning is in progress, early springers which will not spawn for another twelve months, and late autumn fish which will spawn in the next few weeks, may be running in. These are loosely termed winter fish and are not highly regarded. The early springer will be somewhat stale before the next season opens, and consequently be of less sporting and eating value than the spring fish proper. The late autumn fish may not spawn until the main body has completed the act, and so may disturb the redds, destroying eggs already fertilised or exposing them to predators.

The redds are beds of suitably sized gravel and may be situated in the main river, its headwaters or its tributaries. The water flow over them is critical and must normally remain within certain limits for the eggs to survive and hatch successfully.

The female is the key figure in the spawning process. She cuts a shallow trench in the gravel in which she deposits some of her eggs, then moves directly upstream, cuts another, and so on until all her eggs have been deposited. As she extrudes her eggs the male is triggered to extrude his milt close alongside her and so fertilise them. The gravel she disturbs as she cuts each successive trench is washed down to cover and protect the fertilised eggs in the trench below.

After spawning has been completed, the spent female drops down into quieter water. The male fish, especially if all his milt has not been expended, does not do this but remains on or near the redds, possibly to find another mate. In doing so he uses up more energy than does the female and this may account for the high mortality rate among the males after spawning.

Gravid female fish which for one reason or another fail to spawn at the proper time are commonly called baggots and are traditionally ghillies' perks. They are in much better condition than are the spent fish because the act of spawning, which they have not performed, is the most exhausting single enterprise in the life cycle of the salmon, and accounts for about 40 per cent of the fish's loss of condition.

Spent fish (kelts) are protected by law. If caught they must be returned unharmed to the water. Influenced by the release of guanine into their bloodstreams they quickly relinquish their spawning livery in favour of one which has the appearance of uniformly bright tin, in readiness for their possible return to the sea. They nevertheless remain very sorry-looking individuals.

The downstream progress of the kelt is irregular. For the most part it just drops back in stages, and does this more slowly in the larger rivers than in the smaller, shorter ones, but by the end of April most rivers are clear of them. The few that do reach the sea will not travel far and will return to the river as soon as they have regained condition sufficiently to enable them to do this. Not having had the benefit of another sea winter, they are not so valuable for eating as a maiden fish would be.

While all this has been going on, the fertilised eggs will have hatched. It takes from about 90 to about 140 days for them to do this, depending on the water temperature. The newly hatched creatures are called alevins, and each is equipped with an umbilical sac which sustains it for about a further 50 days.

When the contents of this sac have been absorbed, the alevins become fry, and start to feed for themselves. After about six months of doing so they will have developed into the familiar parr.

The parr of one season's hatch do not all become smolts, ready for migration, at the same time. This is another of nature's ways of ensuring the survival of the species.

Parr may spend from one to four (exceptionally five) years in fresh water, at the end of which they assume a silvery coat and head for the sea. This usually happens in May.

As soon as it reaches the sea the smolt starts to feed voraciously. This can be judged from the fact that, from an ounce or two, it can achieve a weight of 5 pounds or more in the space of a single year. From then onwards it is ready to return to its native river.

The compulsions which make the so-called adult fish do this are dealt with more fully in Chapter 3, but it is abundantly clear that it is not merely a matter of sexual maturity. This would not account for some fish returning after only one winter in the sea while others spend up to four winters there. What is more, an examination of the genitalia of returning spring fish shows that in the male there is no milt, and in the female the ova are no bigger than pin heads.

In returning summer fish the gonads may not be very much more developed than in the springers, but in late-autumn fish they certainly are. Moreover, late-autumn fish may have begun to change into their spawning livery whilst still in the sea, and may come in with it substantially in its final state.

This livery is different for the two sexes. The silvery flanks of the male become a copper, red and black tartan, and a thick, yellowy, leathery skin forms over the scales which makes them increasingly difficult to dislodge. Its belly turns a dirty grey colour and its head grows longer, becoming very ugly with a pronounced snout. The point of its lower jaw acquires a cartilaginous kype which projects upwards into a recess in the upper jaw, almost penetrating it. In the period immediately preceding spawning the large male is truly a hideous and awe-inspiring sight.

The female on the other hand remains substantially 'in drawing', merely becoming thoroughly grubby and dingy-looking, with slight traces of red on the gill-covers and possibly a rather coppery sheen to her flanks. Compared with the male she remains reasonably attractive, and her most obvious spawning characteristic is her steadily expanding belly, which eventually spoils her shape.

With spawning, the life cycle has run full circle. Whole books have been written about it, but the foregoing summarises all that the fisherman needs to know. It may also give him a better insight into other environmental and physiological factors when he comes to study them, and so help him to a better understanding of his craft.

3

The Mysteries of Migration

Aided by an imposing array of sophisticated hardware, *Homo sapiens* can now travel vast distances into the unknown with great accuracy. Although many people marvel at this, few give more than a passing thought to the fact that *Salmo salar*, possessing a brain no bigger than a pea, has been doing much the same thing for millions of years, unaided, and that man with all his intelligence still has very little understanding of how the creature does it.

The importance of time as a factor in the salmon's performance needs no emphasising, because on the fish's solution of time/space problems depends the survival of its species. Spawning has to be accomplished in due season, otherwise there would be no certainty that sufficient food awaited the alevins when the contents of their yolk-sacs had been absorbed. To make survival doubly sure, nature also programmes the act to take place in the very area where the fish itself was hatched and where, historically, the survival rate had proved to be adequate. For these and other reasons an inbuilt, versatile clock must exist in every fish, which will enable it to navigate adequately on its long-range journeys and also ensure that all its other actions will be both appropriate and timely.

The operation of this clock is thought to be governed partly by external factors such as temperature, the varying relationships of daylight to darkness and so on, but more probably to depend on a cooperation between external factors and endogenous rhythms. Each fish may therefore have a number of biological clocks to guide it, but whether or not their influences are coordinated in any way – by a single master clock for example – remains as yet a matter for conjecture.

The biological rhythms of salmon are quite well documented and are known to be both circadian, matching a day, and circannual, matching a year. They do not, of their nature, have the accuracy of geophysical rhythms and may deviate from the 24-hour day and the 365-day year to some extent. However, they are never allowed to get very far out of phase with the corresponding geophysical rhythms because of the intervention of certain external signals which period-ically pull them into synchronism.

Apart from their chronometrical nature, enabling a salmon to maintain, say, its compass orientation during migration, the biological clocks provide a means of anticipating coming events – scheduling physiological changes, behaviour patterns, etc., to occur in preparation for, rather than in response to, many cyclic environ-mental events. This anticipatory characteristic is almost certainly influenced by heredity, thus accounting for the different periods spent by fish in the parr stage of development, for the different runs of fish, and for the different periods spent in the sea by fish returning as grilse, 2 +, 3 +, or 4 + salmon.

A pilotage aid, as opposed to a navigational one, is the fish's sense of smell. It is generally accepted that smolts, before migration, have become imprinted with the smell of their particular environment and that it is this which will eventually aid the adult fish in the final stages of its return to its native river. Although its olfactory apparatus is non-directional, it provides the fish with the ability to follow scent gradients and polarised trails to their source. Assuming that the navigational part of its migratory journey has been accomplished with the necessary accuracy, the final run into the correct river will not present a salmon with any particular difficulty.

The salmon's olfactory sense is important to it in other ways too. It enables the fish to be the receptor of numerous chemical stimuli on which it depends for triggering specific reactions, such as the spawning urge. All fish secrete substances (pheromones) which other individuals can receive via their olfactory organs. Some of these substances are species-specific and some, such as alarm signals, are not. The species-specific substances in fact constitute for salmon a means of elementary communication, and it is their existence which accounts for the gregariousness of the fish and its propensity for travelling, resting and feeding in groups.

The main mystery surrounding a salmon's migration reposes in its navigational expertise. Its long, deep-sea journeys differ markedly from the migrations of birds and other animals because, unlike them, it is unaccompanied by path-finders or leaders which have travelled the course before. Smolts begin their migration

weeks after the last kelt has left the river, and it is beyond belief that the two could meet and travel together. Few enough kelts survive to make this a practicable solution and, anyway, it is known that fish which have previously spawned never travel very far from their native rivers before returning to them for a second time.

So it is the problem of the outward journey rather than the return to the river which is the more baffling. Does the smolt have some instinctive goal, or alternative goals? Or is the business much more prosaic, being merely that of following some trail of preferred food until the fish reaches some area where it can happily remain until the time comes for it to start back? It is all a mystery.

On the other hand, the return journey is relatively straight-forward, merely requiring the fish to make good the reciprocal of the outward one. It is not difficult to envisage this as being well within its capabilities, observing that racing pigeons perform a comparable act without much difficulty. How the fish does it is quite another matter.

One possibility is that it employs sun-compass orientation. This is known to play a role in the migration of birds and may also be important to anadromous fishes. The evidence in favour of it is that homing ability is much reduced when vision, combined with the lateral-line sense, is impaired. The evidence against it is that migrating salmon are known to travel by night as well as by day.

Another, more speculative possibility, which would enable orientation by night under variable hydrographical conditions, is that the fish then relies on other celestial cues, but this is a solution which finds litle favour in most quarters.

There is even less evidence that fish can use the sense of smell for long-range orientation.

Finally there is the possibility that salmon can follow a compass course by means of geomagnetic field perception, although there is evidence that during regular journeys of up to a hundred miles to and from a feeding ground fish tend to take different routes from night to night. Nevertheless this solution fills the bill for salmon in a number of ways, and is considered by many to be the most likely one.

Maybe one day we shall know.

4

Salmon and Vision

The basic laws of optics are the same under water as on land. Moreover, the mechanisms of sight in humans and fish are so similar that a salmon fisher may feel justified in assuming that his quarry will view objects exactly as he does. This assumption, while generally sound, has its snags because there are differences which he would do well to keep in the forefront of his mind.

A human being, for example, may be able to observe objects at great distances, if he has an unobstructed view of them. On a clear day these distances may be as great as twenty miles or more, depending on the height of eye. The maximum range of a fish's vision in pure water, on the other hand, is measured in tens of yards rather than miles because of the water's density and its propensity

26

for scattering light (which markedly reduces visual range). Moreover, the environment actually inhabited by fish is far removed from pure water, and this inevitably reduces maximum visual range still further.

A salmon in water which is turbid may, in fact, have a very restricted visual range indeed, and have to rely on senses other than sight for many purposes. In a river, it is forced to fall back on other senses when navigating, or merely maintaining its position and stability, in conditions of darkness or extreme turbidity. A description of these other senses is outside the scope of this chapter, and it is sufficient to say that the fish is able to cope in those conditions because fixed objects in moving water set up disturbances which it is able to detect and locate. It is therefore fair to assume that a salmon is generally far less dependent on sight than a human being would be, and an appreciation of this can be valuable to the fisher.

The salmon fly, for instance, sets up disturbances while being fished which, for a given fly, vary in intensity with the relative speed between the water and the fly. These disturbances will be greater with chunky flies tied on double or treble irons than with slimmer flies tied on singles. When making a choice of fly to suit the conditions, these are factors well worth bearing in mind. By the same token they may help the fisherman to decide whether or not he needs to work the fly when actually fishing with it. In other words he should not necessarily regard a fly's attraction for a fish as being exclusively visual.

Light is the key to vision and, in particular, to the perception of colours. On a dull day a human being will experience greater difficulty in identifying colours at a distance than he would on a bright day. As, in general, the environment inhabited by fish is dimmer than that inhabited by humans, this may be relevant to the colour perception of salmon. What is more, the maximum distance at which salmon may begin to have difficulty in determining colours may be far less than might be expected, and be well within the fish's maximum visual range at any particular moment.

There is, moreover, another factor which may come into the reckoning. This is a phenomenon peculiar to colour perception in water. It is the colouration of the water, as it appears to the fish, as a result of light being scattered by suspended particles and the water molecules themselves. This colouration is called the spacelight, and the colour vision of fish tends to adapt to it.

The combined effects of scattering and absorption cause the

spacelight to vary with depth and with angle of sight. Near the surface (obviously the area of prime importance to the salmon fisher) it is more monochromatic along a horizontal line of sight than along a vertical one, and is at the infra-red end of the spectrum. In consequence it may be that a fish near the surface, observing a white or grey object along a near-horizontal line of sight, will see it as pink. Presumably the hue of objects of other colours may suffer modification in a similar way. The fisherman should not therefore suppose that the appearance of the fly he selects will necessarily remain constant or invariably look the same to the fish as it does to him.

As for the fish's ability to adapt to the colour of the spacelight, this may not help it in light climates biased towards the infra-red as much as it might seem. Fish themselves, and their eyes in particular, radiate in the infra-red spectral region, and it has been shown that this has a fogging effect, reducing the contrast of other infra-red radiations, thus making it difficult for the fish to perceive them. Sensitivity *plus* contrast is necessary for good perception.

Black is the colour which provides the greatest possible contrast with the spacelight near the surface, and a black fly may therefore be the one that the fish is likely to see best in all circumstances. This may account for the long-standing popularity of black flies and for their frequent, often spectacular, successes.

The main way in which a fish's vision differs from that of a human is, of course, that it is monocular, each eye operating independently of the other, with eyes and brain organised accordingly. It has been suggested, although never proved to my knowledge, that the fish is no more able to switch to the binocular mode (if in fact it is able to view any object with both eyes simultaneously) than the human is able to switch to the monocular one. This has a bearing on the way in which it may view objects at close quarters and is consequently a matter of great interest to the fisherman.

In conclusion, it may be as well to examine the hampering effect of dazzle, because this can be a problem for the fisher and he is prone to envisage fish as being equally discomforted by it. Many fishermen firmly believe that a salmon can be severely handicapped in taking a fly by the dazzling effect of the sun when it is shining from some specified direction in relation to the pool. This belief needs to be treated with caution.

The fisherman is handicapped by dazzle, when he is facing the sun and it is below a certain altitude, because its rays are reflected by the surface of the water directly into his eyes as he tries to follow the progress of his fly. The fish cannot suffer in this way because it is beneath the reflecting surface.

On the other hand, when the elevation of the sun is sufficient for its rays to penetrate the water's surface, dazzle could well be a handicapping factor, but it is difficult to believe that it would be so great as to be deemed severe. The fly's path is in the horizontal plane, so the fly cannot come 'out of the sun' in the sense that an aircraft or a cricket ball can. It is only when the fly and the sun are in transit that a fish, following the fly's progress with one of its eyes, would be dazzled. Before and after that point it would be able to see the fly perfectly well. That being so it could easily adjust the moment of the take accordingly, manoeuvring in such a way that it would never have to view the fly against the sun at all.

Moreover the fish's vision is much better equipped to deal with ultra-bright conditions than is the vision of humans, because fish have two sensitivity systems. One is a high-sensitivity system (scotoptic), based on the rods, for use whenever the light level is low. The other, which is a low-sensitivity system (photoptic), is based on the cones. Photomechanical movements come into play whenever required, which shield the highly sensitive rods from the dazzling effect of bright light, and return them to the focal plane of the eye at low light levels.

For these reasons it is very doubtful if dazzle can be as important a factor in salmon fishing as is generally supposed.

5

Other Senses and the Brain

Taste and smell sensors

In fish, both these sensory systems are stimulated by chemicals dissolved in water, where of course the same chemical will stimulate both receptors. Nevertheless there is a functional difference between the two. Taste is essential to the fish in picking up and swallowing food, while, on the other hand, olfactory responses generally vary with environmental conditions and are less capable of being rigidly defined, involving communication, learned chemical cues and the triggers which initiate the urges to feed and to spawn.

The olfactory organs of salmon are comparable to the nasal organs of smell in man, inasmuch as their location and role are generally similar. The fish has a single nostril on either side, but neither opens into the mouth cavity (as in man) so they have flaps which direct water inwards on the forward side of the nostril and outwards on its after side. From these nostrils, nerves connect with an olfactory bulb and olfactory tract merged in the anterior part of the forebrain, usually called the olfactory lobe.

The process is by no means completely understood as yet, but experiments have shown that fish have a very highly developed olfactory sensitivity and will respond, for example, to the smell of their home water when the odour of this is very faint indeed.

There are other organs on the surface of the body, in the skin, on the fins and forming part of the lateral line system, which also appear to be smell or taste sensors, but very little is understood about them.

The main taste organs are composed of taste buds situated on the front of the snout as well as in the roof of the mouth. These taste buds are microscopically similar to those in man, and obviously have to be more sensitive and versatile than in man because the fish often has to rely on them in the selection of food and not merely in the appreciation of it.

Pressure sensors

Pressure sensors are important to fish in monitoring their vertical movements. Fish with swim-bladders are more sensitive in this respect than those without them, and as the swim-bladder is an adapting organ it is reasonable to suppose that a salmon will be principally sensitive to changes in pressure and will not necessarily be capable of accurately assessing depth.

Consequently most experiments with such fish have involved observing their reactions to the application of sudden changes in pressure, quite unlike the gradual pressure changes the fish would impose on itself by vertical movements in the wild: So, although it has been shown that in the laboratory meteorological changes of 20 to 30 millibars should be within a fish's sensibility, it is thought that, in the wild, larger changes than that would pass unnoticed.

The lateral line and hearing

The idea that the lateral line has an acoustic function is a mistaken one. It is now reasonably well established that the lateral line organs do not respond to pressure changes but are sensitive to the displacement component of the propagated sound wave, making it theoretically possible for them to provide a fish with directional information. They appear only to respond to sound under certain conditions favouring large water displacements (i.e. low-frequency sound close to source) which are in the same general direction as the lateral canal axis.

As the lateral line provides the kind of information not available to man, the manner in which the fish uses it is difficult for man to

31

assess. It is believed, however, that by means of its lateral lines a fish can detect minute modifications to its bow-wave imposed by fixed or moving objects (which may be quite a distance away) and that this gives it a sense which has been described as 'distant touch'.

The sense of hearing in fish is provided by the labyrinth, a collective term for the semicircular canals and other associated chambers. As in man, it incorporates the sense of equilibrium, although not in quite the same way. In fish, two groups of receptors are involved, one concerned with accelerations, particularly rotational and directional ones; the other with the direction of the gravitational pull. This combination of dynamic and static information from two different parts of the labyrinth, coupled with that derived from its lateral lines, enables the fish to continue normal activities at night or when visibility is poor.

Whether or not fish actually possess a sense of hearing has puzzled scientists for many years and it was not until modern electro-physiological techniques were developed that its presence was confirmed. As regards salmon, a great deal of extrapolation is therefore involved.

It is known, however, that in addition to being a pressure transducer, the swim-bladder, when linked to the inner ear as with salmon, acts as a sound amplifier, giving the fish a relatively high sensitivity to sound over a wide frequency range, probably well exceeding 2000 Hz.

Recent studies have shown that several species of teleosts (bony fish) can swim towards a sound source, even in the far distant field, without involving their lateral lines. This may be true of salmon also, and is probably not due to binaural cues because of the closeness together of the fish's ears and because both ears are stimulated simultaneously by the swim-bladder. Directional ability therefore requires the inner ear to behave as a velocity- or displacement-sensitive system, because it is that feature of the propagated sound wave which carries directional information. In fact the inner ear seems ideally suited to do this.

Two sound sources 180 degrees apart would, however, have identical response ratios unless the fish could also discriminate between compression and rarefaction. Behavioural demonstrations have shown this to be so, especially in fishes where there is a connection between the swim-bladder and the inner ear.

From all this it will probably be realised that man is only just beginning to understand the accoustic capabilities of fishes.

The brain

A fish's brain is in many respects, and certainly by comparison with the human brain, very elementary. Unlike *Homo sapiens*, a fish cannot reason, deduce, decide and then act; its actions are merely automatic and instinctive. Indeed its brain, which is very small, is very largely bound up with its senses and locomotor activity because of the necessity for the constant maintenance of position and stability. It can never relapse into the condition of sleep, as man knows it.

It has, however, some interesting characteristics. Its component parts seem less specialised than in man, and vital functions are shared among them more than might be expected. When one of these parts is removed in the laboratory, the others appear to be able to make compensatory adjustments. The removal of the fish's forebrain has been found to depress a variety of functions but to eliminate relatively few. The fish might, for example, be found to have equilibrium problems for a while after surgery, but after two or three days these would disappear as other parts of the brain took over.

There would seem to be little doubt of its ability to learn, and a fish will soon begin to avoid some of the things it finds unpleasant or that are liable to endanger it. This probably accounts, in salmon, for the species having successfully survived for as long as it has in the face of all the hazards and catastrophes which have threatened its survival.

6

Salmon and Temperature

Over the years, the folklore of salmon fishing has come to include much that has to do with the thermometer. Many fishermen firmly believe that temperature has an important influence on the behaviour of salmon, and on their taking behaviour in particular. Preferred techniques, and even the patterns and sizes of flies likely to give the best chances of success, have been prescribed in terms of temperature. If this is valid it should fit in with what is known of the environmental and physiological facts, which should confirm that temperature-induced stress or other temperature-related influences will indeed (or as likely as not) compel the fish to act in the way predicted. Where it is not possible to demonstrate this, it is arguable that the fish's actions in this particular context are merely random, and that the theories about them are correspondingly unsound.

In assessing the influence of temperature on fish, two basic facts need to be appreciated. The first is that a fish's metabolic heat production makes no significant contribution to its body temperature. The second is that its body lacks thermal insulation. Consequently a fish is a thermal-conformer, absorbing or losing heat through its body walls and gills so that its body temperature more or less aligns with the ambient.

The process is assisted by the high thermal conductivity and specific heat of water, and is quite a rapid one. If, for example, a salmon is taken from a tank of temperate water and plunged into one containing water near freezing point, its body temperature will align with the temperature of the new environment in a matter of minutes. Only during the alignment process will the fish show marked signs of stress.

Other experiments with salmon have shown similar results, for example that an acute increase or decrease in temperature is required if locomotor activity is to be stimulated, and that the significant factor is the rate at which the temperature of the fish's body is required to change. In the wild, this rate is likely to be low, because there the changes to which the fish is subject will be far more gentle and progressive than in these laboratory experiments. Consequently the stress and/or activity influences of temperature changes in the wild are likely to be minimal.

Furthermore, other than rate of change, there appears to be no causality between temperature and locomotor activity. Experiments have shown that this activity will vary (as between day and night, for example) when the temperature level is held constant, showing that the activity of fishes is not mechanistically controlled by temperature in the general case.

Temperature-induced stress can be come by relatively easily with some species of fish. Tropical fish are a case in point. They will remain stress-free and normally active within a certain optimum temperature range, but have very little tolerance for temperatures outside it and may die if subjected to them for long enough. The salmon, on the other hand, is a eurytherm, i.e. tolerant over a very wide range of temperatures indeed, otherwise it could not survive the wide seasonal changes encountered in temperate rivers where, needless to say, it spends an important part of its life.

The optimum temperature range within which a salmon is likely to remain relatively stress-free and normally active has been assessed, experimentally, as 6°–20°C, but of course the fish survives down to 0°C, aided by the natural antifreeze in its body. As regards the upper limit, few fish can survive temperatures in excess of 40°C, and it would seem that the lethal one for salmon is well below that.

In temperatures above its optimum range it will suffer stress because (inter alia) its metabolic rate, and therefore its oxygen demand, increases with temperature, while at the same time the saturation point of dissolved oxygen in the water falls. In other words, the more oxygen the creature needs because of a rising temperature, the less is likely to be available for it, and ultimately a point will be reached when the fish can do little more than struggle to survive.

The reverse happens at the other end of the scale. As the temperature falls towards freezing point, the fish's metabolic rate and consequently its oxygen demand also falls. Simultaneously the saturation point of dissolved oxygen in the water rises, and at low temperatures the fish is likely to have far more oxygen available to it than it needs. However, another factor then intervenes, because temperatures below 4°C exert an anaesthetising effect on static fish, which progressively increases towards freezing point, and at those temperatures this will be the predominant influence on a salmon's behaviour.

None of this will give much comfort to those salmon fishermen who are temperature buffs, as there is nothing to indicate that taking behaviour can be correlated with temperature. In the optimum range of 6°–20°C, precise temperature levels appear to exert little if any influence on specific behaviour patterns, and the influence of rate of change of temperature in the wild is likely to be minimal also. Furthermore, it seems clear that temperatures outside the optimum range tend towards incapacitating fish, rather than the reverse, and exert an influence on them which is purely negative.

There are one or two constructive deductions to be made, however. One is that the lure should be fished as slowly as practicable and 'got down to the fish' when the temperature of the water is very low, namely below 4°C, because at those levels it will exert its anaesthetising influence, affecting the fish's brain and coordination, and discouraging undue activity. In the optimum temperature range it seems quite unnecessary to do this (observing that the fish would then be normally active) and indeed to be silly to go to the trouble of, say, bumping the lead along the bottom with all the attendant disadvantages of hanking up, disturbing the pool, etc., because to do this would probably be counterproductive in the long run.

The facts also support the view that at very low temperatures salmon should be sought in the quieter lies of a pool, where their dopiness would be less of a threat to their ability to maintain position and stability than it would in the streamier lies.

Although not generally advocated or practised, it may also pay dividends to fish the lure deeply sunk when the temperature of the water is above the optimum range, because that is when fish, finding it increasingly difficult to extract sufficient oxygen for their comfort, might also be discouraged from undue activity. These fish should be sought in the streamier lies, where the ram-jet principle could play a greater part in gill ventilation, and thereby make it easier for them to extract the oxygen they need.

Finally, there is the most widely supported theory of all to be considered, namely that the relationship between air and water temperatures plays a significant and specific part in the taking behaviour of salmon. A case in point is the dictum that the floating-line method should be preferred whenever the temperature of the air is above that of the water, however cold the water might be. This, certainly, is not supported by the facts when the water temperature is below 4°C.

Furthermore, the dictum is difficult to justify on environmental grounds. It is possible, even likely, that a certain relationship between air and water temperatures could have an effect on the behaviour of certain species, such as trout, through an effect on their food supply (always a potent influence on fish behaviour) but that is hardly pertinent if popular belief about the feeding habits of salmon is correct. Moreover, any difference between air and water temperatures will inevitably produce some change, however small, in the temperature of the fish's environment. The influence of this, if it has any at all, can only be towards promoting taking activity in general rather than one or other aspect of it.

So it seems that the validity of the dictum is not supported by the scientific evidence, such as it is. Those fishermen who steadfastly adhere to it, and there is no denying that a very great many do, should recognise that what they are doing cannot, as yet, be justified scientifically and must be classed, in effect, merely as an act of faith.

7

Salmon and Oxygen

Although it is fairly easy to make a determination in the laboratory of the oxygen consumption of fish and of their reactions to changes in environmental concentrations, it is extremely difficult to do this with fish in the wild. Laboratory-based data often require careful interpretation if they are to be useful to fishermen, and what follows is a summarisation in general terms.

First of all it would be as well, if only to get it out of the way, to consider the other respiratory gas which might influence fish behaviour. This is carbon dioxide, which is from twenty-five to thirty times more soluble in water than is oxygen. A fish's ability to eliminate it will therefore always vastly exceed its ability to take up oxygen. Consequently the fish is likely to react to changes in the oxygen supply long before it would to any possible difficulty in disposing of carbon dioxide, making the oxygen supply the dominant factor.

Most fish are either oxygen regulators or oxygen conformers, depending on the way in which they adjust their ventilation rates. Oxygen regulators maintain a relatively constant rate of oxygen extraction, increasing the ventilation rate as the availability of oxygen decreases, and vice versa. Oxygen conformers, on the other hand, do little to change their ventilation rate. Instead they alter their behaviour to adjust their need for oxygen in direct proportion to its availability.

Salmon are oxygen regulators.

Compared with mammals, which have an abundant supply of oxygen available to them in a medium which is relatively light, fish suffer the double disadvantage of having to pump a heavy respiratory medium over their gills and also, because of its comparatively low oxygen content, large quantities of it. This is not always as much of a disadvantage as it might be, because fish in moving water are able to employ the ram-jet principle of gill ventilation to assist them in extracting the oxygen they need and, in that environment, this redresses the balance somewhat.

It is believed that the dissolved oxygen of normally unpolluted river water will be between limits which will enable a static salmon to extract the oxygen it needs without suffering any particular inconvenience unless temperatures are high, just as a mammal at rest will comfortably extract the necessary oxygen from relatively unpolluted air. It seems unlikely that differences in the level of dissolved oxygen between those limits would consequently exert any particular influence on a salmon's behaviour in a river, as it would, say, on that of an oxygen conformer.

The oxygen demand of a salmon varies with its activity, its size, the temperature of the water (as already explained in Chapter 6) and the availability of oxygen. The influence of the first two variables is

39

obvious, and one of the reasons why the last-named becomes a factor is that in hypoxic conditions, that is to say in conditions where there is less oxygen available than is needed, fish appear to be unable properly to maintain the efficiency of their oxygen extraction, especially when hypoxia is severe. This, among other things, restricts a fish's reactions on being hooked to short, possibly sharp, bursts of activity and prevents it from taking out hundreds of yards of line in a prolonged dash for freedom, defeating any skill in playing it that the fisherman might have.

To put the matter in the proverbial nutshell, the responses of salmon to changes in the availability of environmental oxygen produce changes in respiration, blood circulation and other physiological conditions (blood-to-water and tissue-to-blood diffusion barriers, for example) but not, apparently, changes in its behaviour as they would with oxygen conformers. Other than the obvious one that the fish tends to become incapacitated when the concentration is too low for its well-being, its reactions to changes in the level of available oxygen are therefore likely to be of little practical interest to fishermen.

8

A. H. E. Wood of Glassel

Sixty years ago the late Arthur Wood of Glassel stood the world of salmon fishing on its head. No single personality in the history of the sport, before or since, has had such an influence on technique. His method of fishing, publicised by Jock Scott and others, was quickly adopted by fishermen everywhere and employed when conditions were suitable for it. Those conditions, according to Mr Wood, were whenever the temperature of the air was above that of the water. Otherwise he advocated that the fly should be fished deeply sunk and never in mid-water.

There were two good reasons for his method's immediate appeal. The first was that, at one stroke, it made salmon fishing more interesting, more artistic and (because it involved short rods, light tackle and a line which floated) less exhausting. The second was because it was thought to be more productive than the old methods. This belief arose because Cairnton, on the Aberdeenshire Dee, where Mr Wood had been the lessee for a number of years, was a particularly prolific water, even for those days, and moreover happened to be enjoying a run of especially good seasons. Consequently he was killing fish in large numbers. Had he not been doing so it is debatable whether his pronouncements would have provoked the immediate and profound interest they did. As it was, his notable successes led everyone to believe that they were solely attributable to his method. They even fooled Mr Wood himself, who once remarked, 'If the fisherman is good enough, fish will take any day and at least one should never have a blank'. He went on to qualify this, but such dogmatic statements were characteristic of the man. This one is notable because it does not tie in with his habit, common to everyone fishing the middle beats of the Dee at that time, of regarding the season as being over by 31 May. If he fished at all, after that date, he referred to it as 'just fooling about'.

Until his advent fly fishers for salmon had generally employed the sunk fly whatever the conditions. This, it was believed, had to be brought close across the nose of the fish for there to be a good chance of inducing it to take. The preferred technique was therefore to cast a long line well downstream so that it would fish slowly while sinking.

In complete contrast with this, Arthur Wood took the sinking line and greased it so that it floated, and decreed that it should be cast square across the pool, or even slightly upstream. Doing that inevitably resulted in a belly forming in the line which, in turn, had an undesirable influence on the way the fly fished. Accordingly it was necessary for the fisherman repeatedly to remove any belly by 'mending the line', a process to which Mr Wood attached great importance and described at extraordinary length and in great detail.

A technique such as this is exactly what might be expected to evolve when a man restricts himself to fishing for salmon with a short, single-handed rod, as Mr Wood did. There is no need to elaborate on that thought, but his own explanation as to how his method evolved is singularly unconvincing, as fishermen can judge for themselves by reading it in the Appendix to this book. Whether his 'single-handed rod syndrome' resulted from an inability to use a doubled-handed rod adequately, or was rooted in his trout-fishing background and was therefore just a personal preference, remains unclear. He certainly possessed the right physique for it. Not many people are capable of fishing all day with a single-handed 12-foot rod, or for a short while with a 16-foot rod, single-handed, as he

could. Anyway, he did not like double-handed rods
and never used them, as far as the record shows. In
his preference for single-handed ones, and square
casts, he was fortunate in that Cairnton, with its
many croys and comparatively low, clear banks,
was ideally suited for that form of fishing.
Apparently he seldom fished elsewhere.

Using this uncharacteristic salmon tackle he said the aim should
be to keep a small fly fishing in or near the surface, because that was
where it would have its optimum attraction for fish. This could not
be achieved with conventional, fully-dressed salmon flies because
these, fished off a greased line, would skate. So he developed a
range of slimly dressed, so-called low-water flies which were more
appropriate for the purpose and are still in use today.

These he had dressed on long-shanked single hooks as an aid to
good hooking, and he developed his own special technique for
hooking fish. This involved yielding line when the fish took, tightening only after the current had removed the slack and theoretically
exerted a backwards pull. His advice was that the fisherman should
then tighten by swinging the rod, held horizontally, in towards his
own bank. By following these instructions, his theory was that the
fly would end up in the apex of the angle between the fish's upper
and lower jaws (the scissors), where the hook would obtain a better
hold than elsewhere. This, it must be said, was not always achieved
in practice.

Being totally new, his ideas involved him in a great deal of corres-
pondence, and here he was in his element. J. W. Hills, in his
appreciation of Wood which introduced Jock Scott's book about the
new method, said he was just as happy teaching as he was fishing.
Another friend said of him that he seemed to know the answers to
everything. If the cook scalded herself, or a man had a fall out
hunting, or the frost burst a pipe, or the dog bit the baby, he would
know what to do, and everyone would immediately recognise that
he was the proper person to take charge. And so it was with
everything to do with fishing. No matter what the question, he
always had an answer to it and would give this with complete
authority and in the greatest possible detail. In fact from his answers
to correspondents, published in several books, it is clear that detail
interested him quite as much as the broader perspectives and probably more. His answers also show that his views were not always
particularly sound. Sometimes, too, he would resort to the dubious

device of anthropomorphism. For example, one questioner continued to heckle him after hearing him state that the reason why he maintained that his method would only succeed when the air temperature was higher than the water's was because he had always found it so. In the end he said to his tormentor 'If you were in a nice warm hut in the Arctic, would *you* poke your nose out of the door?' – an anthropomorphism which in any case was hardly apt.

There are a couple of questions I would have liked to ask him had I ever had the chance. Given that his aim was to fish a lightly dressed wet fly on a comparatively heavy hook in or near the surface, how could he ever have come to advocate casts which were 'square or even slightly upstream'? These could only result in the fly sinking in the early stages, and so be contrary to his aim. It would have been interesting to hear his answer to that, especially in view of his advice about 'never in mid-water'.

Similarly, those of us brought up in the old sunk-fly-only days know perfectly well that there is nothing new in the concept of mending the line. We were taught to mend it upstream when we wanted to slow the fly down and get it to sink quickly, and downstream when we wanted to speed the fly up and keep it high in the water. The only difference between doing this with a sunk line and doing it with a floating one is that with a sunk line the fisher just has the one chance to do it, which is when the line hits the water. The *effects* are the same, to a degree, whether the line is floating or sunk. In other words, when a fisherman makes an upstream mend with a floating line the fly will cease to fish and sink, if only for a few moments. This is contrary to Mr Wood's stated aim so why, then, did he not only accept the repeated use of the upstream mend but positively demand it? It would have been interesting to have heard his answer to that too.

All this shows that Mr Wood was only human, and not an infallible oracle as many people, perhaps even Mr Wood himself, came to believe. His feet may have had elements of clay about them; nevertheless, he was unquestionably a fishing giant of our time.

—— 9 ——
Mr Wood's Methods Modified

I was one of those salmon fishermen who quickly became a fanatical believer in Arthur Wood's teachings. At first I followed them implicitly, doing everything by the book, but as time passed I began to modify his method, as did everyone else, and as my reasons for this may perhaps have been typical, and illustrate well enough how today's floating-line technique evolved stage by stage, I feel justified in giving them here.

Although I was totally devoted to practising greased-line fishing exactly as prescribed, there were certain absurdities to which I could never quite descend. Some of these may have come about because an enthusiastic admirer had picked up a chance remark by Mr Wood, and had tried to develop it. Some had obviously just been dreamed up. One of them was the business of presenting the fly broadside on to the fish, an idea to which many paid lip service at one time, although I'm sure they did not in the least understand what it meant. I certainly never did. The only way in which it could possibly have made sense was if a fish possessed binocular vision, when broadside on would presumably have meant broadside on to its nose. Anyway I considered it to be all just a lot of nonsense and ignored it.

Another absurdity arose because of Mr Wood's expressed dislike of drag. Again few people seemed to know exactly what he meant and he was in some difficulty explaining it. Anyway, it led to the belief that it was necessary to provide a lot of slack line on the water at the start of the fishing-out process, and devotees set out to achieve this by waggling the rod from side to side while the forward cast was extending. No one seemed to mind that the provision of a lot of slack line would inevitably result in the fly sinking. The whole process seemed so ludicrous that I decided it was not for me.

I cannot excuse myself totally, however, because I was constantly changing the size of fly, as advocated by Anthony Crossley in his book on the greased-line method, and re-greasing the line many times a day, fully convinced that if I did not keep it floating efficiently some mystical attraction of the fly for a fish would have been lost. I need hardly say that I never stirred without a thermometer and took air and water temperatures constantly, loading up the ghillie with sunk- and greased-line outfits so that when Fahrenheit decreed I had the prescribed equipment ready at hand.

Eventually disillusionment began to set in. I think the first things to go were those beastly 'square or even slightly upstream' casts. They were a terrible nuisance, and so difficult to execute without the benefit of Cairnton's clear banks, or Mr Wood's croys. When I had room to execute them, and expended considerable ingenuity and effort in doing so, it was galling to have the fly taken when the line was at a good angle downstream, which would have happened had I made a normal down-and-across cast in the first place. Moreover, I got terribly discouraged by having repeatedly to wade ashore to recover my fly from its lodgment in the tiger country when I had failed to realise that the room was insufficient. Spey casts would have been the answer, but they were difficult to make effectively with the short rods employed at that time. The worst thing was that I seldom had any joy with the fly 'floating' down like a dead leaf, as Mr Wood prescribed. I suppose he must have got fish when it was doing so, but I seldom did. Very occasionally a fish would take at the moment when the fly was starting to fish, and was rising out of the depths like a nymph, but never before that. Anyway I decided that persistent square casting had to go, and it went.

So a stage had been reached where I had gone back to casting more or less down and across while still exercising what I liked to regard as my 'skill' in manipulating the fly by mending the line. One venerable and respected ghillie was very critical of this. When I asked him why, he said that in his experience the principal characteristic which transformed an ordinary lie into a taking lie was the attractive way in which the fly normally fished through it. From this he concluded that it was a mistake to interfere with the fly's normal progress.

Then one day, when fishing with another very experienced ghillie, I twice had the annoyance and embarrassment of mending the line at a critical moment when clearly interesting a fish. As I made the correction there was a boil where the fly was, indicating that a fish had turned away. Of course there is no saying that either fish would have taken the fly anyway, but after the second time it had happened my ghillie friend was exasperated enough to call out 'why can't you leave the line alone?', or words to that effect. He, too, didn't hold with mending in the Wood manner, although he conceded the necessity for making some adjustment to the line, when desirable to ensure that the fly would fish properly, but insisted that this should be done early and then finished with, as in the old sunk-line-only days.

Those two ghillies' criticisms had to be taken seriously, and I began to ponder them in conjunction with a conviction of my own. One cannot hook a lot of fish without coming to notice that the majority take when the fly's position at the time is within certain limits in its arc of travel, and I had become accustomed to regard this as the 'taking arc' where one's chances are best. I daresay every experienced fisherman has this arc in his mind's eye when he is fishing, so I do not claim that there is anything new about it.

To take account of those ghillies' remarks I began to refrain, as far as I was able, from interfering with the fly's progress when it was within the taking arc. This soon became completely automatic, and I believe it has paid handsome dividends ever since. I must add the rider that I am nevertheless prepared to raise the rod at any time if this is necessary in order to lift the line out of eddies or fast water in order that the fly shall cover the lies properly, but when I do so I take as much care as I can to maintain the fly in the fishing mode and not allow it to go dead and sink.

The greatest change in my attitude to accepted greased-line methods came about in relation to Mr Wood's dictum that the floating line should only be employed when the temperature of the air was above that of the water. I began to distrust this, and noticed that a number of experienced fishermen had begun to do so too. A Revised Version of the dictum began to appear, with the amendment that the air temperature *should not be greatly below* that of the water, and for a while I was happy to go along with that because I knew perfectly well that I had been getting fish on the greased line when the air had been colder than the water. In that respect the authors of the Revised Version had been very shrewd. They had transformed Mr Wood's dogmatic and unambiguous pronouncement into one which was flexible and vague. It left to the individual how he defined 'greatly' and therefore left him to interpret the dictum as he thought fit.

Then I had an experience which showed that even the Revised Version did not go far enough. Thanks to the kindness of Colonel and Mrs McHardy of Woodend, which adjoins Cairnton, I was given the privilege of fishing their water all summer (when I am accustomed to fish only the floating-line method). In my determination to learn as much about the water as quickly as I could, I started to get up to fish it at first light. Usually I took good care not to set the alarm unless the evening was cloudy, but one morning in early July, after a succession of boiling hot days, found that the clouds had dispersed overnight. I had risen at 3 a.m. so as to be on the water at the start of morning twilight; had washed, shaved and dressed in what seemed, ominously, to be a very cold room, but it was not until I had opened the front door of the hotel that I realised what I had let myself in for, as there was a really hard frost in progress – the sort of frost you will only find, in the British Isles at that time of year, in northern Scotland. One glance at the river, which looked just like a river of thick haar, inclined me to think that it would be useless to fish, and I very nearly went back to bed. But then I thought I wouldn't and, instead, drove down to Woodend intending to remain in the car until the haar started to clear. However, it was so cold sitting there that eventually I decided to start fishing just to keep warm, although the haar remained as thick as ever.

To cut a long story short, I hooked and lost a fish in the Loop almost at once, and then, later, another at the top of the Long Pool. Now Woodend is one of those delightful beats which has a road along it from end to end. In consequence one could make the car one's base and keep a lot of equipment in it which one did not normally carry. So, for once, I had my spare-tackle box with me. Remembering this, and being sufficiently interested, I made my way back to the car, dug out a thermometer, and found that the air temperature that morning was no less than 20°F below the water temperature.

Experiences of that sort simply cannot be ignored, especially when they are supported by other, similar ones which, although not so dramatic, are, in total, equally weighty. At first I assumed that they showed clearly enough that Mr Wood's dictum was just a lot of nonsense, but that simply would not do because there was the evidence of his records (he took air and water temperatures as a matter of course, often three times a day) to back it up. Then I remembered reading, while researching into the environmental physiology of fishes, that scientists had observed that fishes' reactions to given influences tended to be different at different times of the year. This gave me the clue as to how my experiences of the influence of air and water temperatures on preferred techniques might be reconciled with those of Mr Wood.

His were gained in the spring, when I had little interest in whether or not his method would work, believing rightly or wrongly that the sunk-line method, or the bait, would always out-perform it then.

Mine, on the other hand (and probably, too, those of the fishers who preferred the Revised Version), were gained in the summer, when Mr Wood did not often fish or, when he did, just regarded it as fooling about. In the summer I invariably employed the floating-line method, not because I believed it would necessarily out-perform the sunk-line method but merely because it was the easier, more interesting and therefore the more enjoyable of the two.

So I suggest to any fisherman who wishes to play about with the floating-line method in the spring that he should, by all means, follow Mr Wood's dictum in the matter, but that in the summer, when the floating-line method really comes into its own, he can safely forget all about it.

All that now remains to be covered is Mr Wood's hooking technique.

49

About thirty years ago I became converted to using low-water double-hooked flies for floating-line fishing. These were anathema to Mr Wood, whose hooking technique demanded singles. That is my experience too, because I found at once that with doubles I was just as likely to hook my fish in the roof of the mouth, tongue, jaw or lip as I used to when fishing the sunk fly, when one just waited for the pull and pulled back. Of course I sometimes got them in the scissors, but then I used to with the sunk line too. Now I only employ Mr Wood's method of hooking fish when, in my opinion, conditions require me to employ a single-hooked fly. With doubles I no longer yield line when the fish takes.

I have never been madly keen on Mr Wood's hooking method anyway, for reasons I give in Chapter 17. Too often have I followed the drill to the letter only to find that the line never tightens because the fish is 'awa'. Indeed it is often when the boil has not been observed, and the first indication of the fish's presence is a pull, that the fish has turned out to be most securely hooked.

So what is now left to me, and to the majority of floating-line fishermen today, of the greased-line method as practised and decribed by Mr Wood? Low-water flies, certainly; his method of hooking, partially; but principally the floating-line. What a blessing it is! Every time I use it I give silent thanks for the life of the man who gave it to us.

10

The Lore

The unpredictability of the salmon's behaviour in fresh water gives tremendous scope for speculation and argument. The bibliography of the sport bears witness to this, with successive generations of writers on salmon fishing adding their two-pennyworth. If this had just remained a record of contemporary opinion, well and good, but it did not. Such is the power of the printed word that when some 'expert' had reached some conclusion or other, and immortalised it in print, it often came to be regarded as immutable fact. Other writers then repeated it and it appeared in book after book. Eventually, from sheer repetition, it became installed as part of the Lore, however dubious its authenticity or obscure its origins.

The danger of this process is that it smothers the truth. Once some pronouncement is believed to be fact, the thinking and actions of fishermen tend to conform to it. Conforming practitioners, when successful or unsuccessful in their fishing as the case might be, will then be convinced they have confirmed its validity although it may actually have had nothing whatever to do with either the one or the other. Brainwashed in this way they may never again believe or act

51

differently. What is more, when in the course of time they have experiences which are at variance with a particular conviction it's the odds to nothing they will just brush them aside as of no consequence.

That is how much of the Lore has managed to survive, and how inveterate Lore-mongers are made.

Of necessity, the Lore is full of generalisations which, if their origins were properly investigated, would be found to derive from special cases. One of these – a great favourite among Lore-mongers – is the edict that the fly should be fished as slowly as possible for salmon.

I believe that this had its origins in the days when only the sunk fly was employed, when a theory was current that, in order to induce a salmon to take, the fly had to be brought close across its nose. Everything we did in those days was in conformity with that theory, and to fish the fly as slowly as possible was one of them. The logic of it was this. If one did *not* fish the fly slowly one would have wasted too much of the fishing-out process before it got down to the fish. If, on the other hand, it was fished really slowly it would get down to the desired level early in the fishing-out process, be effective for longer and, one hoped, give better results.

Consequently, I was taught to fish the fly slowly when I began to fish for salmon, because it was essential to do so in aid of the fly-across-its-nose theory. Nowadays it is no longer a part of any theory, yet it still persists in the Lore.

And not just in that form either. One of the things we did, in the old days, in order to ensure that our fly would fish slowly, was to make long casts, well downstream. Not only does the Lore still advocate this for sunk-line fishing but it now includes it in floating-line fishing as well. Observing that a floating line can be manipulated to produce the same effect as a long, downstream cast, there is no logic in this at all.

The implication of the Lore's decree that the fly must be fished as slowly as possible is that salmon are sluggish fish. It conjures up a picture of them as being ponderous and aldermanic, like carp, although nothing could be further from the truth. Our beautiful, streamlined, powerful salmon may at times behave in a deliberate manner (when the water is very cold, for example) but at others can move like lightning. Thousands and thousands of salmon fishers know this perfectly well, but has this had any influence on the Lore? It has not.

If you do persist at all times in fishing the fly as slowly as possible it will actually reduce your chances of success. As spring merges into summer it is quite noticeable that fish will start to prefer the fly which is fished fast. In high summer it is sometimes the only fly they will take. With the river at summer levels it is often quite possible to take up a position from which the fish can be covered with a short line, cast square and unmended. It is educational to watch an expert in this technique at work. Everything else being equal he will return to base, day after day, with more fish than anyone else in his party, and the other members will wonder how he does it.

By all means fish the fly as slowly as possible if that is what you firmly believe to be best. It is good to fish with confidence. And certainly fish it slowly whenever there is a good reason for it, but do not be deluded by the Lore into thinking that it is axiomatic. It isn't.

Another example of the Lore's immutability is to do with the distance one should move downstream between casts. When I started fishing for salmon I was taught that this should be two steps. Again, this was in aid of the fly-across-its-nose theory, and some expert had decreed that two steps, say four feet, was the correct distance to move. Presumably he had calculated that by doing this the fly would, at worst, pass close enough to the nose of any fish for the theory to be satisfied. Anyway, it became part of the Lore.

If Mr Wood did nothing else, he totally demolished the fly-across-its-nose theory, and with it should also have gone this business of taking only two steps down. But the Lore never lets go of anything as easily as that, and you can still read in the how-to-do-it books that one must 'cast, take two steps down and cast again'.

It is difficult to conceive how taking two steps down, as a sine qua non, has managed to survive into the post-Wood era. Regard, for a moment, some hypothetical cases:

Case 1   There is a taking fish lying in 3 feet of water. Someone is fishing over it, à la Wood, and moving two steps downstream between casts. If he contrives, purely by chance, to bring the fly directly over the fish's head, the distance the taker has to move to it is at least 1 yard. If, on the other hand, the fisher has been as far out from bringing it directly overhead as he could be, the least distance the taker has to move is 1·2 yards.

Now take the same case, but with the fisher moving six paces between casts. The corresponding figures are now:

1 yard (same) and 2·25 yards.

Case 2   Everything as above, except that the taker is lying in 6 feet of water. The corresponding figures are now:

Two paces   2 yards and 2·1 yards
Six paces   2 yards (same) and 2·8 yards

Case 3   Everything as above, except that the taker is lying in 12 feet of water. The corresponding figures are now:

Two paces   4 yards and 4·07 yards
Six paces   4 yards (same) and 4·47 yards

So, what have we got? At best there is no difference at all between taking two paces between casts and six. At worst, the taker is being required to move, if the fisher is moving six paces instead of two, by the following additional distances:

Taker in three feet of water   1·05 yards
Taker in six feet of water   0·7 yards
Taker in twelve feet of water   0·4 yards

Can anyone seriously contend that these extra distances, which are 'worst case' figures remember, are so great as significantly to reduce one's chances if one took six paces instead of two? If he does, and prefers to act as the Lore prescribes, he will be taking three times as long to cover the same amount of water as he might have done, and this for a problematical advantage which is marginal at best.

Again, by all means do it if it will help you to fish with confidence, and good luck to you! But it is likely that you will then find that you have got less than your fair share of fish killed in any given period.

Another item of the Lore to which experience has led me to take exception (although many people don't) is that relating to peat water. Reference to this was first made in a book published, I believe, some seventy or eighty years ago, in which the author said that he didn't like peat water because he *thought* it might sicken fish. This was enough for the Lore, which was on it like a flash. From then onwards peat water *did* sicken fish, without question, and for a long time I believed that it did, despite periodical evidence to the contrary. Then, one May, I had cause to doubt it very seriously. I had come up to fish two or three days early, as was my habit, so that I could make a reconnaissance of the water and have a yarn with the preceding party. In this way I was accustomed to ascertain which pools were doing surprisingly well and which surprisingly badly, which it is often valuable to know. And sometimes these friends would be kind enough to let me fish one of their rods for a couple of days, which was fine because thereby I got my muscles working.

This May they had done unusually badly, in spite of the fact that the water was hotching with fish, because the river had been dead low for weeks. There had, however, been a lot of rain just before I came up, and on the day I arrived the river was bank-high and black. By the Sunday it was beginning to fall and their last words to me were that I and my party would be in for a bonanza 'when the water cleared'.

Well, it never did clear. When we started, on the Monday, it was so black that our feet disappeared from sight as soon as we stepped into it. But we had our bonanza all right! It is the best month's fishing I've ever experienced, with fish taken every day from the first to the last, although the water was heavily peat-stained throughout. Every time it started to clear there was more rain and the water turned black again. Never once was there any indication that it upset the fish at all.

If you want further evidence on this point, try reading *Letters to a Salmon Fisher's Sons*, Chapter 12, in which Mr Chaytor describes thirteen fish being taken on fly and bait when, to use his own words, 'the river was black as ink with stained water coming off the peat'.

So what supports the idea that peat water sickens fish, and for so many people to believe it and repeat it, right up to the present day? I think it is this. Immediately after a big rise in any river, peat-fed or otherwise, fish often tend to go right off the fly for a period. In a spate river this may be for just an hour or two. On a more stable river it often lasts for two days, or longer. On a peat-fed river this coincides with the influx of peat water. Moreover, the moment when the fish tend to get back on the fly again usually coincides with that when the peat stain tends to start fading. When the water is black it looks nasty to the fisher, so he concludes that it must be nasty for the fish. Thus, although it is the rise in river which temporarily puts the fish off, the peat water gets the blame. This is the sort of unsound conclusion which is just meat and drink to the Lore.

If peat water did, in fact, sicken fish they would be feeling at their worst after a day or two of it, and be so poorly that they wouldn't want to look at anything, but that is just when they will start to take again. It is also just when the suspended particles of peat are beginning to settle, with their highest concentrations nearest the fish. It doesn't make sense.

It is as well to remember, too, that the fish which the Lore says are sickened are those very same fish which hatched and developed in the acid environment of a peat-fed river, spent up to five years in it as parr and, after one or more winters in the clear blue sea, actively sought it out when the biological urge was upon them. And found it, too, because, inter alia, the particular characteristics of its water attracted them. Furthermore, having found it, the conditions in which they are most likely to be encouraged to run up it are those when the river is big and a heavy infusion of peat water most likely to be present.

I am a fan of the peat water because it is an infallible indicator that the rise in river in which it is present is a true rise, that is to say one emanating from the headwaters of the river and/or its main feeders. This is the rise which has the greatest effect on fish when they have been generally static, reactivating their biological urge and prompting them to move again. If there are fish about, one can usually be sure of several days of good sport, at least, after the river has had a good shot of peat water, especially after a long period without it. On the other hand, a rise due to local rain, when no peat stain is present, has only a problematical effect, and if it does result in an improvement in sport this is usually slight and short-lived.

I don't deny that there may be some rivers where the fish will react as badly to peat water as the Lore makes out. All I can say is that I have yet to encounter one, although I have fished one or two where it is alleged that this is so. My experience in these is that if conditions favour good sport the influx of peat water will not necessarily spoil everything, and that if sport has been bad the influx may well have a beneficial effect.

A few years ago I was fishing one of these rivers when there was rain in the hills and its water turned black. We were near the end of our time, so an American member of the party, advised by the ghillie that it would be quite useless to continue to fish, decided to pack up and return to the States. The other members of the party, similarly discouraged, went off to fish for trout elsewhere. I had a good beat, so I stayed with it. At the end of the day the trout fishers returned empty-handed, but I had had a nice fish on the fly.

I hope these few examples will be sufficient to show how generally harmful it is to become a Lore-monger. I could easily add to them, giving instances of fish being taken immediately before and during thunderstorms (which may put trout off the take, but certainly not salmon), and during gales, and in blazing hot sunshine, and when the water was particularly frothy, and in downpours, and when the sun was shining down the pool, and in haar, and at night, and so forth, contrary to the Lore. If you are a Lore-monger your confidence will be sapped in such conditions and, as confidence in what one is doing is an important contributor to success, you will suffer. You will also influence others, either directly or by example, and may cause them suffering too. I will, however, relate one more story, because it sums up so neatly the Lore's propensity for making fools out of salmon fishermen, however experienced or otherwise competent they may be. It was told me by the ghillie concerned.

A couple, both first-class fishers, came down to the river one morning, before lunch. The husband went off to start at the top of the water and his wife, accompanied by the ghillie, proceeded to a pool some half a mile below, near the hut.

When he arrived at the top pool the husband saw that the river was full of flotsam, and obviously rising. He started fishing but soon became discouraged. 'This is no good!' he said to himself, and after a while decided that he would be better employed at the hut, with a gin and tonic.

On his way there, he passed his wife, fishing. 'You're just wasting your time,' he called out to her. 'Don't you know that fish will not take in a rising river?'

The ghillie turned slowly and looked at him. 'Wee-ll,' he said, after a pause, 'we've had three, anyway!'

—— **11** ——

Dubious Theories Explored

Although not strictly part of the Lore, there are a number of dubious theories and beliefs about salmon behaviour which seem to have been current since time immemorial. Some of them are clearly illogical, some even weird, and most can be shown to be unsound by applied commonsense, by observation, or by what is known of the relevant physiological and environmental facts. Yet they persist.

At the root of some of the weirder theories is the fish's lateral canal system. This has no counterpart in man, and until recently very little was known about it or the information it provided. Consequently it commended itself to anyone setting out to construct an explanation for anything seemingly inexplicable.

It has been credited, for example, with giving fish supra-normal perception; that by means of it they could detect that the river was rising before any rise had actually occurred in their vicinity.

It is perfectly true that fish seem sometimes to anticipate a rise, and be stimulated into running or taking hours before it reaches them, but there is no way in which this could be by means of their lateral lines. These organs can only register conditions local to the fish, and to credit them with any ability beyond that is to enter cloud-cuckoo-land.

If any explanation has to be found for fish running and taking in advance of a rise, it probably lies with their senses of smell and taste. These are known to be extremely sensitive, and able to detect changes in water flavour which are minute.

Supporting this idea is the fact that the behaviour which seems so mysteriously to anticipate a rise is seldom to be observed before one due to local rain, and brought about by an added influx of land drainage water and road washings. It is usually only to be observed when the rise originates in the headwaters of the river and/or its main feeders – areas where the main spawning activity occurs. It is not therefore, in all probability, the rise itself which is the stimulating factor but rather the predominance in it of a certain type of water. If this is the factor which stimulates the fish by, for example, intensifying or reactivating their biological urge (as I believe is so) they could well detect and react to a change in the balance of the water's constituents before any noticeable rise had reached them, and so give the impression that they were anticipating it. Whatever its other merits, this is a more down-to-earth explanation than the other and a more credible one.

Those who think that a rise in river level will, of itself, stimulate the activity of salmon often believe that unsettled weather similarly will stimulate them, and that by means of their lateral lines they can detect its approach before any local change occurs. The two beliefs are incompatible, however, because the theory advanced for fish anticipating unsettled weather is that they do so by detecting that the barometer is falling. Leaving aside any question of their ability to do this, no fish could differentiate between barometric and water pressure, i.e. water height. A fall in barometric pressure would therefore be registered as a fall in water level, the opposite of what was supposed to stimulate fish, according to the first theory.

In any case, it is by no means established that fish do in fact anticipate bad weather. It may be just an old wives' tale.

59

Another theory which can be seen to be dubious is that relating to the timing of the early spring runs. It is to the effect that the sea temperature around the British Isles in winter is fairly constant at around 42°F, and that if river-water temperatures are below that figure the fish will wait about in the sea until these have risen to a more comfortable level. This, on the face of it, is quite a reasonable theory – indeed Calderwood supported it at one time – but it is not confirmed by observation, as Calderwood eventually admitted. Spring fish can be seen to be running into northern rivers when the temperature of their water is well below 42°F, and to refrain from running into others where the water temperature is on a par with the sea's, or higher.

A number of factors might govern the springers' behaviour in this respect but the predominant one could well be river level. When this is high, the influence of the outflow from a river will extend many miles out to sea. It is possible to have visual or other evidence of this as far as seventy miles off the mouth of a major river. The greater the outflow from a salmon river the greater the chance, therefore, of its anadromous fish finding the water they are seeking and being influenced by it. As the original theory does not fit the facts, this one is a possible alternative.

Another theory not supported by observation is that fish running early in the season, when the water is very cold, are held up by major obstacles in a river, which normally they would be perfectly capable of surmounting, because they will not face the white water associated with them. It is true that such obstructions do sometimes hold up running fish early in the season but it seems doubtful if this has anything to do with the white water. Fish in northern rivers in winter or early spring can be seen to have faced and passed through white water associated with minor obstacles, or none at all, so it seems probable that it is the obstacle, rather than the white water, which can hold them up. A reasonable alternative explanation is that it is their biological clocks which are the influencing factor. The fish have plenty of time, nearly a year in fact, before they have to reach the redds and the compulsion to exert themselves in sur-mounting significant obstacles could, as yet, be lacking. This ties in with the evident truth that running springers normally progress up river far more slowly than do summer or autumn fish, and this could well be because more time is available to them than to the others before they have to fulfil their biological purpose.

Another fallacious belief about white water is that fish like to move into it when the water temperatures are high because it is more highly oxygenated than the water elsewhere. It may well be highly oxygenated, and fish may well move into it in high summer, but the one cannot be consequent on the other. Those who believe the two to be connected seem to be confusing oxygenation with aeration, imagining that water with a high oxygen content can give up oxygen as easily and quickly as aerated water gives up its air bubbles, but that is not so. Water will only give up dissolved oxygen when it becomes saturated with it and there is then a rise in temperature or a decrease in pressure. Consequently it is quite erroneous to think in terms of small pockets of highly oxygenated water in a river. They could not possibly exist there in isolation.

An alternative explanation for fish moving into white water in high summer is that they do so to obtain cover or shade. This seems to be a far more reasonable one than the other. Fish may also move into streamier water (white or otherwise) when water temperatures are high, for the reasons given in Chapter 6.

One of my personal beliefs, held very firmly for a number of years, was also eventually observed to be misconceived. I had thought that fish would always stem the current once they had entered a river. I had realised that they would probably drop back for considerable distances in spates, until they had found suitably sheltered lies, but not that they would actually swim downstream on occasion. Then for about ten years I fished where there were a number of vantage points from which the behaviour of fish could be observed when conditions were right, and took full advantage of that. Apart from being very impressed by the hitherto unrealised amount of fish activity periodically to be seen, I also, on three occasions, saw fish swimming downstream until they went out of sight. When they do this they go at such a pace that it is extremely difficult to see them and impossible, I would guess, with the naked eye. But my observations were customarily made through binoculars. It was almost by accident that I saw the first fish on its way downstream. A shadow just flicked across the field of view, and by swinging the binoculars I happened to pick it up and discover that it was a fish. Perhaps there is far more downstream movement in a river than we think. It would certainly explain why the upper reaches do not become jam-packed sooner than they do, in view of all the running activity (upstream) to be observed during the season.

It seems to me that the sounder salmon fishing theories are those based on the two things which have the greatest influence on fish behaviour – the biological clock and the biological urge. Springers, for example, would press on until they reached the redds if their biological clocks did not switch off the urge to procreate until the proper time for this arrived. In the interim, the two influences seem to be nicely balanced. Sometimes something will occur which temporarily results in the urge overriding the clock, allowing the fish to make a further move towards the redds. When the temporary influence has abated the clock takes over again, and movement is halted. This theory may be dubious because it has never been proved, but taken in conjunction with others it can explain a lot. A suitable story with which to end these reflections is therefore the following one, because it illustrates how strong are the biological influences on salmon behaviour (and, incidentally, that fish may sometimes swim downstream).

A salmon was taken in a trap in a tributary of one of Scotland's great salmon rivers. As an experiment, it was tagged and transported for about thirty miles up the main river and there returned to the water. Two days later the same fish was found in the same trap.

12

Canadian Interlude

About forty years ago I spent a while fishing for Atlantic salmon in the Canadian Maritimes. It was a chance opportunity, so I had not had time to do any homework and didn't know exactly what to expect other than that the fishing would be fly-only. I had no salmon tackle with me, just New Zealand trout tackle, and was worried about my guide's reaction when he saw it. I knew from past experience of Scottish ghillies that if he didn't approve of it the consequences could be somewhat abrasive. Also I was still weak from abdominal surgery, and thought I would probably be too unfit to do more than token fishing, especially if the wading was bad. In other words the portents were not particularly favourable.

To my surprise and relief, everything turned out splendidly. Even my tackle was right. In fact my guide was most respectful because, he said, I was the first Englishman to employ him who had turned up properly equipped. I was careful not to tell him that this was just an accident.

As for the fishing, how can I best describe it? Imagine, if you will, fishing every pool in ply in the Spey from Craigellachie to the sea, and you will get some idea, because I did the equivalent of that *every day*! No strenuous exercise was involved, and practically no wading, because for most of the time I was sitting in a canoe and was only put ashore in order to play out and land fish. With my health as it was, nothing could have worked out better.

Apart from being a thoroughly enjoyable experience it was also a fascinating one. I was steeped in the conservatism of the Old World, with its folklore and traditions, and this contrasted sharply with the thinking and attitude of many Canadians to many of the sport's problems. Untrammelled by a similar handicap to mine, their views were often refreshingly new. Although I did not realise it at the time, they were going to start me thinking about salmon fishing in a way I had never done before. Until then I had always accepted blindly everything I had read or been taught. Since then I have needed to be convinced that it was sound before being prepared to accept anything.

The first conflict between the views of the New World and the Old occurred almost at once. My guide was playing a very acrobatic fish, and every time it leaped he raised the rod vertically, at arm's length, over his head. When the fish had been landed, I expressed my surprise, saying that I had always been taught to lower the rod point when a fish jumped. This, in turn, surprised *him*. He didn't think it was sensible to lower the rod point because by so doing the natural ability of the rod to absorb jerks was surrendered. What is more, holding the rod high when a fish came out of the water would often, with the greased line, lift the line out of the water's embrace too, making the shock-absorbing qualities of the rod even more effective. I couldn't argue against the logic of that. So much for the Lore's 'Always bow to a leaping fish'.

This particular conflict of view was quickly followed by another. Every morning he would telephone around to discover where the best fishing was likely to be, and decide where we would start that day. Then a truck would arrive, and our canoe, tackle, food and dry sticks for a fire would be loaded into it, and we would set off for the place he had selected. On arrival there, the truck would be unloaded and sent away with instructions to the driver to meet us at a suitable point some fifteen miles or so downstream.

'Why cover so much water?' I asked. 'Surely it would be better to select two or three of the best pools and spend the day fishing them?' He explained, with commendable patience, that the more water we covered the more fish we were likely to get, everything else being equal. Having been brought up to regard one or two pools, carefully fished, as constituting a good half-day's fishing I was not to be convinced. Today, with many more years of experience behind me, I know that he was absolutely right.

One day, when things had been rather quiet, we temporarily suspended our progress down river because he wanted to show me something he thought I would find interesting. So we landed and made our way up to a small bluff. There, in a pool below, was the greatest congregation of fish I have ever seen. The pool was absolutely packed with them. We watched them for a time, and then he must have noticed the gleam in my eye because he said, 'It's no good fishing for them, you know. They won't take anything whatever you might do. You could waste days on them without getting so much as a pull. If I were to let you try we would have the rangers after us, because the only way of getting one would be to foul-hook it. When the time comes for those fish to move on it will be quite a different matter, because then we shall have the most tremendous sport. It's such a pity that you will have gone before then.'

I think this encapsulates a fundamental lesson which every salmon fisher needs to learn. The mere presence of fish is not enough. To provide sport they must be fish of the right kind, that is those which are (if the anthropomorphism can be forgiven) in the right frame of mind. Those are the ones which are important to a fisherman, and which he should make it his business to find. The others will just be wasting his time if he concentrates on them.

Another thing my Canadian guide did for me was to give me an insight into the potentialities of pausing fish. At that time I was staying at a fishing camp on the Miramichi, and there was another man fishing from the camp that week. One day his guide came over to say that there were fish lying just above a nearby footbridge over the river, and that it would be as well to cover them before they moved on. We went up on to the bridge to look and, sure enough, there was a fish of about 15 pounds lying there in full view, with two smaller fish lying a few yards below and to one side of it. This was clearly a situation which was familiar to both guides and one for which they had a well established drill. The other guide and his rod embarked in their canoe and moved out into position. My guide and I remained on the bridge, and the rod, under my guide's direction, proceeded to lengthen out line until his fly was covering the larger fish. Everything could clearly be seen and this is the only occasion in my life when I have been able to see, and watch, the fly while it was actually fishing.

While we watched, the rod made cast after cast. Sometimes the salmon dropped back a foot or two as the fly passed overhead and sometimes it appeared to ignore it altogether. It was quite interesting at first but eventually I became bored and asked my guide if we could not get on with our own fishing. He ignored me. After a while I repeated the question, but more strongly. 'We've wasted ten or fifteen minutes in trying to get that fish to take. Surely that's enough? It's obviously not going to do so!' This made him a bit cross, and he accused me of not wanting the other chap to get his fish. He explained, patiently enough, that this was a place where fish merely

65

paused, and if we could hit off the right moment there was a good chance that one would take. This was an idea which was quite foreign to me. I had been taught by the Lore to regard plastering a fish as one of the cardinal sins.

I don't know how long it was before things started to happen. It seemed to have been about half an hour, and a stage had been reached in which even the guides felt inclined to give up. But then one of the two smaller fish left its lie and started to wander off upstream. This information was relayed to the canoe. Then, suddenly, as the fly described its customary arc the other small fish rose slowly from the bottom, moved forward in a curve to meet it, and was hooked. After the disturbance had subsided there was no sign of the larger fish. 'Well, you've learnt something!' my guide said. I had, but at that particular moment I wasn't sure what it was. I suppose that is an example of the 'delayed action' aspect of experience.

There was no delay in my reaction to another event, however. We had arrived back at the camp one evening to find someone fishing below the footbridge on the other side of the river. He was an old man and waist-deep in the water. My guide regarded him with obvious affection, and told me he was a local character who had done nothing but fish all his life, and made his living from it. 'We call him the Fish Hawk,' he said. 'Would you like to meet him?' I said I would, so we went over to the footbridge and started to cross the river. Before we had got to the other side the old man was into a fish, and by the time we had reached him he was already wading ashore with it on his gaff. It was quite a big fish, 18 pounds in fact, and the whole process had taken about two minutes.

I thought it was a simply staggering performance, and said so. 'Oh, he just charms his fish on to the gaff!' said my guide, laughing, but the old man would have none of that. 'Provided you keep absolutely still', he said, 'and don't put any pressure on the fish, you can often "con" it into coming within reach. You must be prepared for it, if it does. It's no good unslinging your gaff at the last moment or it'll be off like a flash. You should try it some time.'

66

I did try it, a year or two later, on the Awe, and was promptly broken, much to the ghillie's disgust. But I realised that, in the process, I had ignored one of the cardinal rules about playing fish on the fly in heavy water and so could hardly blame the old man's technique for the disaster. I have since found his tip to be extremely effective in the right circumstances, but please do not imagine that I advocate trying to emulate what he did in its entirety. It is just that the ability to con a fish towards you, immediately after you have hooked it, is a really useful weapon to have in your armoury, and it is not at all difficult to acquire. In the old man's words, 'You should try it some time.'

So, one way and another, the Canadian interlude was a great success. It had been a lot of fun, I had enjoyed some good fishing and, at the end of it, my health had much improved. I cannot remember ever having been so lucky with any other fishing trip undertaken out of the blue on an impulse, nor one on which I learnt such a variety of things which have stood me in good stead for so much of my fishing life.

13

Difficulties with Dialect

There was only one slight blot on the otherwise Elysian trip to Canada and that was that I ran into dialect trouble. Even in the British Isles this causes problems in certain localities. It is not just that it makes normal social intercourse difficult; it also carries with it the danger that the native of a given area, who can only speak in dialect, will be hurt or offended if you cannot properly understand him. This may damage a potentially friendly relationship, or at least get it off to a bad start. Naturally I am usually on my guard against that.

I soon forgot all about it on this occasion, however, because I found that I had no difficulty whatever in understanding my Canadian guides. Their speech was like that of West Countrymen, and, as I had spent some of my early years in Devon and Cornwall, there could hardly have been a more familiar sound in my ears.

It therefore came as a great shock to my sensibilities to discover that they could not understand *me*! One of them took me aside on my first evening, after we had had a few tinctures of Seagram's V.O., and told me in the kindest possible way that they found me practically unintelligible 'because of my twang'. In those far-off days I prided myself on the clarity of my diction, so I was cut to the quick. It brought home to me in the most exemplary manner what it feels like to be dialectally handicapped, and I didn't like it at all.

Since then I have done my best, when faced with dialect, never to let on that I am in any difficulty in comprehending it. The need to avoid hurting another's feelings seems to demand this. It also demands that a special effort be made to become familiar with any dialect likely to be encountered, and this is what I am normally at pains to do.

In beautiful Aberdeenshire, where I have spent many enjoyable

68

fishing seasons, the dialect has me completely floored, however. This is hardly surprising because it floors many a Scot as well. It contains words which went out of common English usage two hundred years ago, or more, and the pronunciation of the remainder camouflages them to such an extent that, to an average ear, they are just about impossible to make out.

I had a friend, a Don-side farmer, who used to take time off from his harvesting to pop over to see us when we were fishing nearby. While he gave me his latest news all I could ever do was nod or shake my head from time to time, as seemed appropriate, because I could only identify the occasional word. Sometimes I had quickly to change a nod into a shake, or vice versa, having detected from his expression that I had chosen the wrong one. When I was totally at a loss I would resort to 'A-a-a-ach!' All this gave me a great feeling of guilt, which I mitigated to some extent by plying him with frequent drams.

The rest of my party, all Scots, fared no better. One of them, after a long one-sided conversation with my Don-side friend, was asked 'What does he do?' After some thought the reply was 'Well I don't really know, but I *think* that at one point he made some reference to "the hearse". Maybe he's an undertaker.' This only goes to show, because a more unlikely candidate for that sombre profession than Ben in his working clothes, with his weatherbeaten countenance, cloth cap and collarless shirt (to say nothing of the half-bottle of warm jungle-juice in his hip pocket), would be difficult to imagine. His remark about the 'hearse' was, we discovered later, merely some reference to his harvest.

As a general rule it is only women, in Aberdeenshire, who are bilingual. Mercifully most of them are. When I lodge in the village, or at a farm, I would feel painfully isolated but for that. As it is, I can enjoy some social intercourse with husbands, brothers and sons because of the good offices of their womenfolk as interpreters.

An exception to this rule is Dee-side's foremost fly tier, rod builder and tackle maker. He *has* to be bilingual because his clientele is drawn from 'locals' and 'foreigners' in almost equal proportions. His workshop is, moreover, a social centre where all sorts of people connected with fishing, or the river, tend to gather to pass the time of the day. It is quite fascinating to hear him switching from one dialect to the other, as circumstances dictate. For example I have sat listening to him having a long conversation with the head water bailiff without being able to understand one single word. Then he turned to me and I had no more difficulty in conversing with him than I would with, say, a native of Inverness, where the spoken word is reputed to be the purest in the land.

It does not do to be over-confident, however, and on one memorable occasion he caught me napping.

I was returning home after an unsuccessful and particularly frustrating day on the river when I decided to look in on Willie to have my batteries metaphorically recharged. I found him alone in his workshop and sank gratefully into one of the chairs provided. After we had talked of this and that for a while I understood him to say 'You should have come in earlier, because I had three owls in here, all at once'.

I was amazed. 'Good heavens,' I exclaimed, 'in day-time too! How on earth did *they* get in?'

Willie looked at me cautiously, showing the whites of his eyes. 'Why through the door of course. How do you suppose?'

This seemed fair enough, because there was no chimney to the hut, and none of its windows looked as though it could be opened.

'Well,' I said soothingly, surveying the piles of everything, everywhere, 'they don't seem to have made much of a mess. Obviously you managed to get rid of them very efficiently!'

It was Willie's turn to be amazed, but then the penny dropped. 'Not *owls*!' he cried, 'EAR–R–R–RLS!'

After that there was nothing for it but to buy a whole heap of his beautiful 'flees' in the hope that this would act as balm for his possibly wounded spirit.

14

The Right Fly

Those of us who have read *Days and Nights* will remember that Scrope starts it with an imaginary conversation between himself and his friend Mr Lobworm, to whom he confides his intention to write a book on salmon fishing.

'You really had better do no such thing,' Mr Lob replies; 'why the subject is utterly exhausted; ninety-nine books have been written upon it already and no man was ever the wiser for any one of them, although many are clever and entertaining and, moreover, abound in excellent instructions.'

Scrope had a delightful sense of humour, and obviously loved to write with his tongue in his cheek, but I would guess that he also had a serious intention when he chose to introduce his book in that particular way, especially if he had fly-fishing principally in mind when he did so. Books on that aspect of the sport are, in fact, often clever, entertaining and instructive, but if anyone expects to experience some blinding revelation through reading them he is, by the very nature of things, expecting too much.

After all, fly-fishers for salmon set out to tempt the unfeedable with the uneatable which, of itself, is bizarre. What is more, their efforts have always been purely empirical, and empirical solutions to any problem become properly valid only when they have been confirmed by controlled experiment. That is impracticable under fishing conditions. All that can be done with a fly-fishing technique is to judge it on how well it appears to work and, with salmon fishing, appearances can be deceptive. Little can therefore be taken as the ultimate truth, only as contemporary opinion, and the accepted practices of one era can become discredited the next. This indeed has happened over and over again. Take the development of the salmon fly as an example. Opinion about salmon flies has con-

71

stantly changed through the centuries and although at any given time there have always been people who were convinced they had found the right magic, in the end they have always been proved to be wrong. History shows this only too clearly, and it is useful to survey it with a critical eye because this can so often illuminate the present and, perhaps, give one a glimpse of the future.

It is generally accepted that the development of the salmon fly dates from the trout flies of *The Treatyse of Fysshynge with an Angle*, written in the fifteenth century. The only reference to it in that work is: 'Ye may hap to take hym but hyt is seldom seyn with a dub.'

In the sixteenth and seventeenth centuries it is clear that fly-fishing for salmon continued to be distinctly unpopular, and very little of any sort was written about it. Mascall, in his *Booke of Fysshing*, repeated more or less verbatim what had been written about it in the *Treatyse*, and Walton merely wrote of the salmon that 'he is very seldom observed to bite at a minnow, but sometimes he will, and not usually at a fly'. Another writer condemns salmon fly-fishing as 'not worth the patience'.

By the end of the seventeenth century, however, specific dressings for salmon flies began to appear. Franck and Chetham mention them, the latter favouring gaudy dressings with up to six pairs of wings, which are generally assumed to have been dragon-fly imitations.

In the eighteenth century, the process of imitation was taken several steps further, with mayflies, stone-flies and even horse-flies mentioned. By the end of the century a true lure was also emerging under influences from Ireland.

It was not until the nineteenth century, however, that the popularity of fly-fishing, as a method for salmon, really took off. This was a time of conflict between the comparatively quiet fly patterns of the mainland and the gaudier Irish lures. From that particular battle the latter emerged victorious, and were favoured because they were 'found to be so successful'. Consequently numberless patterns of brilliantly dressed flies came to be created.

At the end of the nineteenth century, Kelson appeared on the scene. His avowed intent was to produce 'scientific' order out of the prevailing chaos, and it is clear that he had convinced himself that his system would enable a fisher to select and employ a 'right fly', whatever the circumstances or prevailing conditions. To support his arguments he made observations about the way of a salmon with a fly which were truly penetrating, but no one who embarked on a

72

critical review of his book could fail to note that the conclusions he drew were so biased and illogical as to be worthless. For example, he wrote: 'Men call salmon "capricious", but is not the term a cover for their own ignorance about the habits of the fish and the flies they show them, rather than the truthful representation of the facts?' No one would quarrel with that statement, but it does not provide grounds for believing that there is such a thing as a 'right fly', which would, in a given situation, produce the desired result, as Kelson went on to deduce. It could equally well be argued that fish might take a fly not because of its precise nature but in response to entirely different influences. Indeed that is a view of the problem which many fishers, today, prefer.

Another of Kelson's observations rings such a loud bell that it must also be mentioned. He wrote: 'If he [the salmon] is as immobile as the rock of the river bed today, and gives himself away to the rawest novice on the morrow, depend upon it there is an underlying cause which it were more profitable to seek for than to cover up with the convenient term "caprice".' Again, this is a most significant and profound truth, and had he not been so obsessed with his hobby-horse he might have drawn sounder conclusions from it. He might at least have admitted the possibility that apparent capriciousness could just as well be accounted for by the effect of changing conditions on the fish as their effect on the appearance and seductiveness of the fly, but he does not. On the contrary he uses it to support his 'right fly' theory, and ends his instructions on how such a fly should be selected with the words 'And is it not indeed an achievement to present to the fish a fly that he then and there prefers to your rivals' – to have yourself made the attraction so strong as to establish, more or less permanently, a decided taste in the fish so that he refuses other flies *to wait for yours?*'

To that question I can only reply 'No comment'!

In due time, Kelson's 'scientific' system was found not to work, and some other solution to the persistent capriciousness of salmon had to be found. It was now the turn of those who believed that correct presentation needed to be given at least as much attention as the employment of 'the right fly', and the fly-across-its-nose theory was born.

As already described, this theory was to the effect that a fish could only be expected to take 'the right fly' if this was brought closely enough across its nose. Technique was modified accordingly, and salmon fishermen sought to fish the fly as slowly as possible in order

73

to get it down to the level of the fish as early in the fishing-out process as possible, with that object in mind. As a theory, it had one inbuilt advantage, namely that a failure to bring the fly close enough across the nose of the fish could be held accountable for any remaining capriciousness observed.

The twentieth century began with a swing away from the complicated flies of Kelson and Gribble. Changes introduced by Crossfield and Pryce-Tannatt were more or less designed to make fly dressing simpler and more economical in materials, but it was Chaytor whose ideas foreshadowed what was to come. His advocacy was towards fewer patterns and that these should be of a much more primitive type. This heralded a move towards the 'bare essentials only' concept, which characterises salmon-fly dressings today.

Then came Arthur Wood. His advent was rather like that of the Demon King in a pantomime – explosive! He totally demolished all remaining remnants of the fly-across-its-nose theory because his method demonstrated that fish could, and actually did, move several yards to take. He showed, too, because he was forced to use them, that flies which were even simpler and more lightly dressed than Chaytor's could be as effective as any. Hence the modern tube-fly which, in many instances, is dressed with merely a few hairs.

Finally we come to the present day, in which it has recently been shown that the so-called low-water flies of Wood, together with primitive tube-flies, can be just as effective when fished off a sunk line as they are when fished off a floating one, and that large flies with complicated dressings are not necessarily demanded even when fishing deeply sunk.

Wood and his contemporaries were, it must be said, just as convinced that successful fishing depended on finding 'the right fly' as any of their predecessors. Because of the decline in the importance of pattern, only one alternative remained open to them – to pursue and emphasise the importance of size. Their predecessors had regarded this as being of no particular significance and to be properly related only to water levels. Kelson, for example, specified what was to be taken as 'the full-sized fly' and avocated departures from it only when water levels were unduly high or low. Wood's contemporaries, on the other hand, evinced a preoccupation with size which rapidly became almost manic. Anthony Crossley, who had a close contact with Wood, averred that depth of water was of no importance in choosing the right size, and that choice should be

74

based on a number of other factors – pace of water, water temperature, the nature of the water surface and the light.

Indeed, theories as to what size of fly should be used in given circumstances became exceedingly difficult to justify. It was maintained, for example, that a change from, say, a No 6 to a No 7 could be crucial in inducing a fish to take, yet it was at the same time accepted without question that the size of the hook, alone, could be relied upon as an effective size indicator. Nowadays only the more gullible fisher accepts that, or really believes that flies of different types or patterns, tied on a variety of different sorts of hook, will appear identical in size so long as their hook size is the same.

Furthermore, a given fly passing 12 feet overhead must inevitably appear smaller to a fish than the same fly passing 6 feet overhead; nevertheless depth of water was held to be irrelevant. This was just as well, when you come to think of it, because the depth of water in a pool is far from constant because of irregularities in the river bottom, and changes in depth would be hard to identify.

Moreover, even if it is to be believed that fish are connoisseurs of size to the extent that a micrometrical change in it can bring about some magical metamorphosis and induce them to take, who can be sure that to make such a change will enable him to take advantage of this phenomenon? Consider for a moment what happens when fishing the floating line. The fisherman aims to avoid allowing the fly to skate or, insofar as he is able, to sink. For most of the fishing-out process it therefore presents two images, the direct and the reflected one, which are to a greater or lesser degree connected. It is the juxtaposition of these two images which, most probably, conveys to the fish the impression of size. The position of the one in relation to the other is, however, constantly changing, and does so in response to changes in speed and other vagaries of the current. It also changes with the angle from which the two images are viewed. In consequence the impression of size conveyed to the fish is continually varying, and the whole enterprise is vague and imprecise. It is anybody's guess what effect some small change in fly size would have on it, and very doubtful if to make such a change would have any worthwhile effect whatever.

Be that as it may, fishermen nowadays are reluctant to accept the proposition that fish will detect, and react to, changes in fly size of the order advocated. In the main they prefer to select a fly which, from experience, they know to be a 'reasonable' size for the conditions obtaining, and stick to it. In practice, the size which is deemed to be reasonable varies so much from one successful fisher to another that it shows clearly enough that there is really nothing crucial about size at all.

On the evidence, it is extremely unlikely, therefore, that a pre-occupation with employing some closely defined 'right size' of fly is any more soundly based than was Kelson's preoccupation with a 'right pattern'. Certainly we are no nearer to finding the right fly than ever we were (given that there is such a thing) and Mr Lob's words continue to carry conviction.

If Arthur Wood was a successful revolutionary, there were others who were not so successful. His method found favour everywhere, but dry-fly fishing for salmon, pioneered in North America by Hewitt, La Branche, Lee Wulff and others, did not turn out to be so exportable. The advantage claimed for it was that it would enable an angler effectively to extend his 'season', but that proved to be a false hope in Scotland at all events, as Lee Wulff was to find out. I have seen it employed there many times, but only once successfully, and that was against a group of head-and-tailing fish which had resol-utely survived a prolonged attack à la Wood. In Canada I never saw it employed at all, and my guide did not once suggest that I should give it a try, although he knew perfectly well that I was equipped to do so. I can only conclude, rather hesitantly, that in the context of the main tree of salmon-fly development, the dry fly is no more than a minor offshoot, and that the wet fly, by means of which all the significant water within reach is covered with every cast, remains of paramount concern.

How then are we to make sense of it all, observing that salmon remain obstinately capricious after five centuries of attempts to find the right medicine? What is more, how could certain beliefs which have failed to stand up to the tests of time ever have come to be so firmly held by so many people with so little justification?

To take the second question first, it is possible to be thoroughly convinced of the validity of any salmon fishing theory if it is put to the test only when chances of catching fish are good. Fly-fishing for salmon, in particular, is not very productive at other times, and that needs to be understood by those who wish to get full value from it. It is possible that salmon fishers of the fifteenth, sixteenth and seven-teenth centuries had not properly appreciated this point and, in consequence, had labelled the method as 'not worth the patience'. By the nineteenth century, however, it had certainly been appreci-ated and from then onwards, up to the Second World War, most fly-fishers for salmon (and particularly the experts) confined themselves to fishing at the 'best times'. This was a perfectly practicable thing to do because there were far fewer people fishing in those days than there are now, and the availability of good water at such times was not out-run by the demand.

A classic example of this was the customary practice on the middle beats of the Aberdeenshire Dee, which embrace Cairnton. When I first went to fish there the 'season' was deemed to be over by 31 May, although the actual season extended into the autumn. After two or three successive blank days towards the end of May the ghillies were prone to announce 'They're through', implying that it was no longer worthwhile to continue to fish in this fly-only stretch of the river. By the end of the month all the rods would have packed up and gone home. As far as they were concerned, that was the end of it, even though they were leaving behind a river which was well stocked with fish. The run was over.

There is evidence, too, that a similar situation obtained on other rivers where there were no fly-only rules. Fishermen would only fish the fly when the run was on. At other times they would employ other methods, for example 'Naething but the prawn!', to quote the immortal words of the late J. J. Hardy's ghillie. No wonder that practitioners of diverse fly-fishing techniques could delude themselves into thinking them tried and true if they only tested them when they would probably succeed!

As for making sense from the lessons of the past, a first step might be to admit that everyone might hitherto have been barking up the wrong tree; that, by putting all the emphasis on searching for the right fly, fishermen may have been blinding themselves to influences which were far more fundamental.

Contemporary experience lends weight to that view. The demand for good fly water since the Second World War has been increasing at such a pace that it is no longer practicable for the majority of salmon fishers to confine their fly-fishing activities to the 'best times'. Fly-only rules on many rivers, and the difficulty of getting on to a good water at any time, force many to fish the fly when chances of success are not good, whether they like it or not. This has paid unexpected dividends in their understanding of the sport, because they have noticed certain features of it which, perhaps, escaped their forebears.

The most fruitful place for such observations is the predominantly spring river. On a predominantly autumn one, no one is likely to consider that fishing is really worthwhile until the main runs start because, until then, the river will have no worthwhile stock. The river which has good spring, summer and autumn runs is also not particularly fruitful because the contrast between fishing at the 'best times' and others, on such a river, is insufficiently great for much to be learnt from it. One 'best time' merges with another, and definition is blurred. On a predominantly spring river, on the other hand, the 'best time' is well defined, as on the Aberdeenshire Dee, after which the fish population tends to become static and the chances of catching fish on the fly become relatively poor. That gives an angler who continues to fish it after the best time is over a special insight into fish behaviour, and enables him, if he fishes through the summer and cares to experiment, to make a far better judgement of the validity of the 'right fly' theory than pre-war fishermen were ever equipped to do.

He will find, for example, that as soon as the tail-enders of the spring run have passed through his water the sport he has been enjoying falls off dramatically, even though his pools remain well stocked. He can try every pattern or size of fly under the sun, fish floating or sunk, and put into practice every theory which ever existed but nothing will improve it. Sport will not remain uniformly bad, however, because every now and then there will be a sudden change which appears to be spontaneous and, for a period, maybe for two or three days only, it will improve. If he has a good stock of fish it may even become just as good as when the original run was on. After this spasm there will be a relapse, and sport will decline again to its former dismal level until the next spasm occurs.

If he is fortunate enough to be able to fish on until the autumn he will notice something else. Whereas improvements in sport during the summer have been spasmodic, with spasms which may be few and far between even in the best years, there comes a time in the back-end when sport suddenly improves and remains good for the rest of the season. In other words, the spasms have been exchanged for a steady state, rather similar to that obtaining in the spring, although most of the fish now involved are stale.

All this has to be accounted for, and if he is thoughtful and observant he will note that, although he can do nothing which actually promotes sport, there is always one common factor present whenever it is good – fish movement. Other factors such as weather conditions, water temperatures, river levels, and so forth have no consistent bearing whatever, except insofar as they affect this. If he tries to take account of them in any other way he will soon find himself drowning in a sea of contradictions and confusion, as so many have done before him. On the other hand, if he sticks to fish movement as the only common factor he will remain on firm ground. Fish are clearly moving in the spring, when the main flood of fish enters the river and proceeds upstream. He can see that they are also moving during the summer spasms by the sudden appearance of new fish in his pools or by observing, from some appropriate vantage-point, that something has triggered some fish to move and that they have temporarily resumed their progress up river. He can also see that fish are moving again during the back-end steady state, when the full biological urge has been reawakened in them compelling movement towards the redds.

Once it has been accepted that good sport with the fly goes hand in hand with fish movement in a predominantly spring river (and there are now countless fishers who have had the opportunity to observe this and bear witness to it), is it not reasonable to suppose that it does so on other types of river as well, even though it may not be so easy to observe there? It would be difficult to prove otherwise, should anyone wish to do so.

From that premise has developed the latest theory, which many salmon fishers believe to be the most convincing one yet. I will discuss it in more detail in the following chapter, but in brief it is to the effect that taking periods are a function of fish movement; that some moving fish will take the fly readily for an indeterminate period after they have paused to rest. After that, when they have paused for long enough, it will become virtually impossible to get them to take a fly again until they have become unsettled preparatory to resuming their progress upstream.

This theory accounts quite well for many things that it is possible to observe. It accounts for the fact that fish which will take artificials are comparatively few at any given time, but are not necessarily always far between, as anyone who has happened to hit on a group of pausing fish will appreciate. It also explains why sport with artificials becomes so bad when the fish population becomes generally static, and improves immediately fish show a tendency to start moving again. It also fits in nicely with traditional convictions about fish behaviour, for example that natural baits such as prawns and worms, which appeal specifically to a fish's sense of taste, must necessarily be employed against resident or potted fish if there is to be any chance of interesting them.

79

Its main impact on technique is that it postulates that fish which will take artificials at any time are phenomena in their own right, and cannot be created purely by divining and employing some mystical 'right' fly, devon, spoon or plug. The corollary is that any reasonable one will do and that instead of fiddling about with pattern or size the angler should concentrate his efforts on finding the taking fish. He should not, therefore, say to himself at the beginning of a day's fishing 'There are x fish in my beat, I will go out and induce one to take' but rather 'There is one taking fish in my beat, I will go out and find it'! And then, if and when he has been so lucky, 'There is another taking fish in my beat, I will go on and find *that*', and so on. In other words it demands a change in strategy.

Although, as I say, this is a theory to which many fly-fishermen now subscribe, there are those who shy away from it because they feel that it denigrates too much the importance of personal expertise. They *like* to think that skill in fly selection has paid dividends for them in the past, and refuse to admit that this skill may have been spurious and illusory.

Is their's a fair criticism? Well, the presumption that to find the taking fish should be the paramount endeavour does not in any way preclude anyone from continuing to try to find the 'right fly', as in the past, if that is what he feels compelled to do. All the theory suggests is that this may be just so much wasted effort, a contention which, it must be admitted, past history appears to support.

If advocates of the 'right fly' theory do want to persist, it would seem that they really have no place to go. All the possibilities seem to have been exhausted. In that connection there has been rather a sinister development recently, and that is a revival of interest in flies dressed to the old patterns. Can this mean that empiricism has run full circle, I wonder? I hope it doesn't, because the prospect of having to slog our way through the whole process yet again is something I, for one, wouldn't wish to contemplate.

15

The Taking Fish

W. J. M. Menzies, at one time Inspector of Salmon Fisheries of Scotland, author of *The Salmon, its Life Story* and other books, was probably the most respected authority on salmon of his time. Even today, fishermen will say 'If that was what Menzies said, it's good enough for me.'

One of the things he said was extraordinarily imprecise, however, namely that salmon do not feed in fresh water. That was over fifty years ago, and it may be that in those days it was not generally known that salmon do, in fact, feed in fresh water. Landlocked Atlantic salmon, which are a feature of the North American scene, certainly feed in it, or they would have died out long ago. Recently, plantings of well established landlocked Atlantic salmon eggs have been made in rivers flowing into Lakes Michigan, Superior and Ontario and, although it is still too early for much to be known about their progeny, it is clear that they feed in the Great Lakes and show no propensity whatever to migrate to salt water. The salmon's disinclination to feed on its return to its native river is therefore nothing to do with fresh water itself.

Very little information is as yet available as to what these salmon feed on in the Great Lakes, but it is probable that they subsist mainly on smelt and crustaceans (crayfish and freshwater shrimp) as do the New Zealand steelheads which treat Lake Taupo as their 'sea'. When the steelhead runs were on I have had great sport with the locally dressed smelt fly in the rivers flowing into Taupo although, in common with many species bent on spawning, the steelheads had probably ceased feeding in the true sense before they started to run.

Another respected authority on Atlantic salmon – W. L. Calderwood, author and contemporary of Menzies – was guilty of a similar imprecision. He, too, was at one time Inspector of Salmon Fisheries of Scotland. He did find food in the stomachs of salmon in fresh water on occasion, but in his view this did not invalidate the general case. It was he who made the classic remark 'If a man meets me at four funerals in a dozen years, is he to conclude that I make a habit of going to funerals?' He never sought to provide a convincing explanation for food being found in some fish after they had entered fresh water, and I suppose thought his quip was enough.

Mr Wood, who had as inquiring a mind as anyone at that time, did endeavour to find an explanation although I understand that he supported Menzies and Calderwood as to the general case. Having observed (as I have done) groups of salmon taking surface fly – March Browns – he persuaded himself, and a great many others as well, that fish took fly into their mouths in order to crush them and extract the juices. Moreover, he said that he had found traces of these juices in the vents of fish he had examined.

He followed this up by assigning to a friend, a local doctor, the task of examining the stomachs of all fish killed at Cairnton over a period. I was privileged to talk to this gentleman some years ago and naturally asked him what had been the outcome. He told me that no food had been found in any of them, but that in one there had been a piece of gorse. He volunteered the opinon that this find indicated clearly enough that some fish were prepared to ingest some things in fresh water, and thought it quite possible that they ingested insects (which the gorse would have represented). He also thought

82

it possible that they had the ability to evacuate the contents of their stomachs in spontaneous reaction to some events, and that the fish with the piece of gorse would have had difficulty in doing this, which accounted for the gorse's presence.

Many famous fishermen have had similar convictions, and have backed them with solid evidence. Traherne, for example, stated that three grilse caught in Norway were found to be gorged with insects – apparently daddy-long-legs – and that Norwegians sometimes found half-digested food in salmon.

Hewitt watched a group of salmon taking surface fly, caught one with an artificial, found natural fly in its mouth and a 'yellow substance' filling its stomach.

Sir Herbert Maxwell, on seeing a salmon take a white moth or butterfly, promptly took it with a Mayfly. He said there was no doubt about its 'gustatory intent'.

I need not labour the point. Hardly a year goes by without there being some evidence, somewhere, that the cessation of feeding by salmon when they regain their native rivers is by no means absolute. Nevertheless when any fisherman tries to point this out, the examples he cites are invariably, with diabolical humour, dismissed as 'red herrings'.

Red herrings or not, and despite the very evident loss of condition of salmon in fresh water, it seems that too many anomalies remain unexplained for the pronouncements of Menzies and Calderwood to be accepted without question. None of the doubters has ever claimed that fish intent on spawning retain an appetite for food in any way commensurate with that possessed during their sea life, yet it is advanced as evidence in favour of the contention that fish cease completely to feed in fresh water that rivers would rapidly be cleared of everything edible if they did not. I imagine that the assumption here is that they would be cleared of all small fish, but the small fish in many salmon rivers are the young of the *Salmo* genus, and species-specific pheromones would see to it that they remained unharmed. In my many years of fishing for salmon I have hooked thousands and thousands of parr (*salar* and *trutta*) in or near salmon lies and never once has one been touched by a salmon. But a spoon of a similar appearance will be taken readily by the same fish.

It is also true that the fly life in many salmon rivers is extremely prolific, with tremendous hatches to be observed at times. If fish were disposed to feed on these flies to a limited extent the inroads they would make on the fly life of these rivers would be virtually undetectable.

Because of the contention that salmon cease feeding altogether when they enter fresh water, explanations as to why they take artificials had to be concocted, but none of them has ever been in the least convincing. It has been said that they do so 'from aggression', but no explanation is ever forthcoming as to why a salmon should be so aggressive towards a bunch of worms trundling slowly towards it along the bottom, while at the same time displaying none at all towards buzzing or wobbling baits swinging past its head. Neither does aggression explain why the fish should pick up the bunch so delicately, carry it into quieter water and then proceed to engorge it. Moreover, in all the hours I have spent watching salmon I have never, except at spawning time, seen salmon display any sign of aggression whatever. On the contrary they seem to be extremely placid creatures, content to live in close proximity with their fellows and smaller fish, without being irritated in the slightest degree. It is noticeable too, that it is only the male fish which displays aggression as spawning time approaches. Why, then, does one hook so many females at that time?

Then again, curiosity has been advanced as an explanation, or that a reflex action prompts a fish to take. All these are characteristics which a normal fish would possess all the time. Why then do so few in any given number of fish, take? Why also does that miserable, emaciated travesty of a salmon – the kelt – apparently display a curiosity and a keenness of reflexes, which are so superior to those of a fresh-run springer in all its glory?

The scientists stand pat on the fact that, although the stomachs of salmon taken in the sea are often found to be full of herring or other marine food, those of fish taken in a river seldom contain any solid food at all. Superficially this seems convincing and conclusive, and obviously Menzies and Calderwood thought it so. But is it? For one thing, no one as far as I know has ever sought to take into account the differences between the two environments. Seawater is alkaline, but the water of most salmon rivers is acid. Might that not make a difference to digestive and evacuatory processes? Migratory fishes are known to drink water in large quantities while in the sea, but to drink very little when in fresh water. Eels, for example, drink at less than 5 per cent of their seawater drinking rate when they return to their rivers. The drinking rate of migratory rainbows similarly alters, and it is reasonably certain that this is true of salmon too. These are factors about which much has been discovered in recent years. Might they not also be relevant?

Finally, what a salmon in the sea can do with a stomach full of herring and what it might be able to do in fresh water with one containing a mishmash of small creatures like insects and shrimp might be quite different. Has anyone ever considered that?

Anyway, I really could not care a fig about whether it is true that salmon, as a general case, cease feeding when they re-enter fresh water, because as a fisherman I am only concerned with why they take my fly. It seems to me to be only common sense that they take it as food and for no other reason, whether or not ingestion is actually intended. In this I am at least supported by the philosopher Occham who, in his celebrated Razor, stated the general proposition that whenever faced with a problem to which there are a number of possible solutions the simplest solution is the one most likely to be correct.

As regards where takers lie, this is naturally bound up with where salmon in general are to be found. Many fisherman seem to look at this from a very limited viewpoint. A river is not necessarily just a moving body of water confined between two banks. If it is wide it has what mariners know as its deep-water channel, which, in effect, is a winding river within a river. This can be broad in some places but is often quite narrow. In some places, on the outside of a bend for example, its position is obvious, but in others this is not so if you don't know what to look for. When it is narrow, its position is given away by the 'stream' – the band of faster water running through the remainder – and an angler should always look for this when fishing a pool because, when the latter is in ply, it will give him an idea of where fish in it are probably lying. The lower the water level the more the fish will tend to be concentrated in the 'stream', or close to its edges. In higher levels they will spread out more, in the same way as the stream itself will then spread out. Only in a really big water may they be found anywhere.

This deep-water channel may not be very much deeper than elsewhere. I remember, when I first came to fish a certain pool, being told that there was a deep gut running down the centre of it in which the majority of fish would be lying when it was in ply. Some years later, when the river was at a record low level, I set out to discover exactly how deep this gut was, and found that it was no more than three or four inches deeper than elsewhere, and that I could wade across it. But there was no doubt about its influence on the fish. Most of them would be found in it in normal conditions.

An appreciation of the importance of this 'stream' in judging where takers may be found is far more useful to someone fishing a pool with which he is not very familiar than any preconceived notion of the type of lie they might prefer. Again, very parochial views about this are commonly held, which are often unfounded and misleading. Over the years, I have made a point, when a river is low, of investigating lies from which I have taken several fish in order to see if there was any common factor other than that to be attributed to the stream, and have eventually come to the conclusion that fish will lie just about anywhere that happens to be comfortable for them in the prevailing circumstances. In very heavy water they may sometimes take advantage of the 'ease' which may stretch for thirty yards or more downstream of a big boulder, and if one can identify its limits from surface indications this can often be a fruitful spot. In general, however, it doesn't seem to matter whether the bottom is of rock, shingle, gravel, sand or mud. It is all the same to them provided that it is firm. They will lie in scoops located in otherwise unprotected expanses of shingle, or behind shallow, rounded stones embedded in the bottom, just as readily as elsewhere. It is impossible to identify such places from surface indications, and if some 'expert' says it can be done I'm afraid I just do not agree with him.

The answer to the question of *when* fish will take is best found in identifying, and explaining, non-takers, which always seem to be in the majority in a salmon river. I have some convictions about them.

The first is that some fish will never take the artificial fly at all. This is not something which is susceptible to proof. All I can say in support of it is that if, when parr, they are hooked by a fly-fisher, dragged unceremoniously through the water and lifted out of it into an unfamiliar and potentially hostile environment, to be shaken or even handled, it is likely to be an experience so traumatic that it would be imprinted on them for the rest of their lives. My conviction may not therefore be quite so far-fetched as it might seem. It may be that some fish will never be disposed to take a fly because they have been strongly conditioned against doing so in their parr days.

My next belief is that fish will not take while actually running. It is one of the few pronouncements of the Lore which, my experience tells me, is unquestionably true. I know that there are one or two people who think otherwise, and are convinced that they have actually hooked running fish, but I think they are merely deluding themselves. I have never been able to hook one myself, although I have tried to do so often enough.

Possibly the most convincing evidence on this point was revealed to me during the years when a friend and I rented a certain water for the season. I cannot tell you its name for obvious reasons. Its records were bad, and the official explanation was that the water had been lightly fished, but someone in the know told me that the real reason was that fish tended to run through it, or such was the local belief. There was talk that it was the effluent from a nearby town which caused this, but I don't think that could have been the whole story. Anyway, the rent was low, so we took the water, and in those days I had the confidence of youth and reckoned that where there were fish I could catch them.

In the event we did unbelievably badly, season after season. At the 'best times', the beats above and below us would be having tremendous sport, but we would not, however hard we fished. There was a bridge across the river, about half-way down our water, from which we could see the fish meandering up, in their twos and threes, but even when we then concentrated on the adjacent pools we would not get an offer. One day, when a guest was fishing the pool below the bridge and I the one above, neither of us having had a touch, the ghillie insisted that I came up on to the bridge to see for myself that this was not due to any lack of fish. I did so, and watched forty fish passing through in a matter of twenty minutes or so.

Then, one afternoon, I went to a pool not far from the bridge and got three fish, one after the other. After the third one, the ghillie and I went on to the bridge to see what the situation was, and in the half-hour we were there never saw a single fish pass.

It is not just my experience on this water which has convinced me that running fish do not take. On another beat I know very well there comes a time, each year, when fish will no longer lie in a particular stretch even though this is usually the most productive one of all earlier in the season. From that time onwards this stretch simply is not worth fishing, although there is no doubt that fish pass through it in considerable numbers and sport in the pools above remains as good as ever. When we did fish it we would have blank day after blank day, even when its pools were in perfect ply. It is now no longer offered for rent in the latter half of the season.

My third belief is that a potted fish – one which has remained static for a long enough period – will not take a fly until something, a reawakening biological urge perhaps, unsettles it and inclines it to move on. In contrast with other fish, those which have become potted have become uninterested in virtually everything, and it seems reasonable to suppose that their interest in food would have become minimal too. Certainly if you have 'naething but residents' in your water it is normally a case of 'naething but the prawn or the worm' if you are to stimulate any of them to take. These are bonnes-bouches to a salmon and I think that the behaviour of potted fish provides telling evidence that salmon in a river are still interested to some extent in food, whether they actually intend to ingest it or not.

All these convictions make their particular contribution as to why there are always so many non-takers about when one is fly-fishing. I need hardly point out that they also fit in most significantly with the theory about taking fish, as briefly described in the preceding chapter. If you are convinced, as many salmon fishers are, that neither running fish nor potted fish will take the fly, only pausing fish remain as possible takers. Similarly, if you believe, along with many salmon fishers, that some fish will never take the artificial fly at all, and those which remain as possible takers are influenced by an interest in food, which is likely to vary from fish to fish according to circumstances, and not by some other, inherently constant, characteristic, the conclusion is that a proportion only of these pausing fish will take at any given time, just as the theory postulates. On these grounds alone the theory appears to be sound.

The test of any theory is, however, how well it fits the facts. If it does not explain adequately what can be observed, it should be discarded in favour of another which does so better. This one fits them neatly enough and, at the risk of repeating some of what has already been said in the preceding chapter, it is worth reflecting on how well it does it.

Not only does it explain why a water's best catches are likely to be recorded during a period when a flood of fish is normally moving through it, that is to say a 'best time' with rents correspondingly high, but it also explains why sport, then, can be so variable and is not merely dependent on the number of fish moving through. For example, one is never likely to do so well when fish are belting up river, everything else being equal, as when they are running slowly. To account for this on the grounds that fewer fish may be pausing in the former instance than in the latter seems reasonable enough.

The theory also accounts for the fact that when the first frosts come and fish which have been static during the doldrums of the summer in a spring river are stimulated by the reawakening biological urge to start moving again, the improvement in sport can be so dramatic. Often enough it becomes just as good as during a 'best time', even though most of the fish now involved are stale. This has been particularly marked recently, and could be because UDN has died down in the warmer water conditions of summer and, by September, is no longer influencing fish as it did earlier in the season. Consequently they are proceeding at a more normal pace. In these and other ways the theory can be tested and its validity confirmed.

It follows that anything which promotes movement of fish will be good for sport and anything which discourages or inhibits it will be bad, but this has to be viewed in its proper perspective. It is not totally useless to fish the fly when conditions are such that the fish population is generally static, and there appear to be 'naething but residents' in one's pools, because there always remains the possibility of encountering the odd maverick fish which is determined to run, no matter what. It is difficult to understand what it is that impels certain fish to do this, but the phenomenon certainly exists. Often enough, when one hooks such a fish, one finds that there is something wrong with it which may be affecting its well-being and so threatening its prospect of survival to the redds. Anyway, I believe that mavericks constitute one's only prospect of having sport when conditions are generally against fish movement, unless one is prepared (and permitted!) to resort to the prawn or the worm. And possibly even then.

All this leads to the conclusion that however skilful a salmon fisher may be with the fly, and however comprehensive his local knowledge, success is only partially due to this. For the remainder one has to look to the fish. It is rather like success on the racecourse, 10 per cent due to the jockey and 90 per cent due to the horse. In fly-fishing for salmon, however, I'd put it as 25 per cent fisher and 75 per cent fish.

This is such an important point that I am going to labour it still further by taking the case of a reasonably proficient and persistent salmon fisher who is enjoying poor sport with the fly. He will inevitably look for the reason. If there are insufficient fish, this will obviously account for his lack of success, and will satisfy him. If, on the other hand, there are plenty of fish about, but he is not hooking any, he may be tempted to blame this on a number of things: air temperature or barometric pressure being too high or too low, peat stain in the water, easterly or gale force winds, the brightness or oppressiveness of the day or on a hundred and one other things which might spring to his mind. In my view he is ill advised to do so because, although some of these things may be relevant to the taking behaviour of non-migratory species or those which truly feed in fresh water, they are irrelevant to salmon. When sport is good he will find that none of them matters a jot, if he will only take the trouble to notice. So few people do! They never seem to think it strange, either, when the conditions they consider so adverse do not seem to be affecting the river as a whole, and that beats elsewhere may in fact be doing quite well.

If he is not doing well when he thinks he ought to be, the reason for it, in all probability, is that too few fish are moving and, of these, too few are pausing in his water. Alternatively, if there are plenty of fish moving through, it may well be that too few are pausing anyway. This may be because of UDN, which tends to make fish travel faster and further than normal, or it may be because his water happens to be lacking in residents. Fish are gregarious, and when they do not find company in a pool tend to press on up river until they do. Or it may merely be because their pausing pattern at this particular time in the season does not include his water, which they are leap-frogging, and that he has 'naething but residents' which have not yet received an impulse to move.

In other words I would implore him to 'think salmon' and not in terms of other species, as too many salmon fishers are prone to do. This may not help him to be more successful, but at least it will have kept his feet on the ground.

Finally, I am bound to say that when I actually find a taker, and reflect on what this has meant in terms of being in the right place at the right time, I have an overwhelming feeling of having participated in a minor miracle. In all the years I have been fishing for salmon, nothing has changed that!

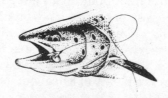

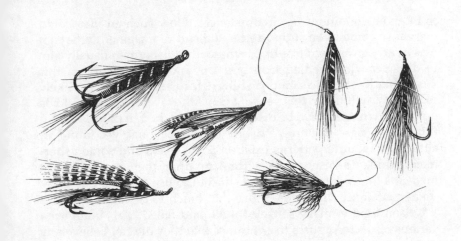

16

The Reasonable Fly

For more years than I care to remember, I have been convinced that the 'right fly' concept had no sound basis. I have given some grounds for this belief in Chapter 14 but as the concept is an unconscionable time a-dying it might be as well to recapitulate and reinforce the arguments against it.

Firstly, pattern. There are hundreds of patterns of salmon fly which have been popular for a while but none of them has ever been other than empirically based. When, in the dim, distant past, people began to fly-fish for salmon they merely took existing trout patterns and tied them on much larger hooks. Then variations were introduced which, to put it bluntly, were just dreamed up. If these variations took fish (and, let's face it, pretty well anything will sometimes) it was thought that they must be good and they became popular. The more they were used the more they were seen to take fish so they became standard. A significant aspect of this is that, when they had had their day, most of them vanished into obscurity.

At the same time a belief arose that a 'right pattern' could be found to fit given conditions or circumstances. How such an idea could ever have come to be supported is difficult to imagine. Perhaps it was a carry-over from trouting, where trout fishermen usually aim to discover what feeding trout are 'on' and imitate it. If so, this would hardly apply in salmon fishing, because salmon are not likely to be 'on' anything, in that sense. Even if they were, there would be no way in which it could be discovered or matched. If there is such a thing as a 'right pattern', no one (praise be!) has yet found it, although favourite patterns exist on some rivers and some fishermen delude themselves into thinking that they are the right medicine (or, indeed, the only medicine) to use there. If this gives them confidence, however, it has that much to be said for it.

Kelson tried to make sense of it all, and failed. This influenced various respected figures to announce that they did not believe any pattern to be superior to any other. The Lore immediately pounced on that and, before you could say 'knife', we were all being told that pattern did not matter and that it was size which was the all-important feature. For a long while that has remained the accepted theory and, since Mr Wood, it has been carried to ridiculous lengths. We have even been given guidelines as to the size of fly to be used in different water temperatures; told that this should be regarded as the basic fly to be used in medium-paced water, and that flies of a size or two larger or smaller should be used in faster or slower water, as the case might be.

There was never any sound basis for any of this. No evidence that, if you did as prescribed, you would fare any better than anyone else. As I have said before, such evidence would only be forthcoming if trials confirming the proposition had been carried out in controlled conditions, and none has, nor is even practicable. It was all just a quirk of the imagination on somebody's part. What is more, the whole concept is probably optically unsound, as suggested in Chapter 14. Size may be one thing in the mind's eye of the fisher but quite another in the eye of the fish.

Although salmon will take the dry fly and, on occasion, other inert objects in, or on, the water, the consensus is that an impression of life is probably the wet fly's most important characteristic. In a fast-running, rocky river, any wet fly starts off with a great advantage in this respect because the river itself, with its many ripples, eddies and eases, confers life to some extent. Because of that, Mr Wood was able to take fish with a bare, painted hook, but that is not to say that dressing is unimportant or that life need not be simulated in other ways too.

A modern dressing does this by creating the impression, when the fly is in moving water, that it is vibrating or pulsating, or both. The impression of vibration is given by the action of the water on wings, tail and stiff hackle; that of pulsation by its more subtle variations acting on long, soft hackle, or hair. In the eyes of the modern fly-fisher for salmon, a wet fly's dressing can therefore be very simple indeed, provided it has been created with these points in mind. Logically, the precise pattern, the choice and arrangement of colours and textures, is immaterial, as past history tends to confirm. Its only importance probably resides in its effect on the fisher, and the extent to which it gives him confidence that the fly he has selected is likely to succeed.

Wings, tail and hackle are not endowed with energy, however, so their vibrations and pulsations are not originating signals which travel outwards through the water as would the movements of a live creature. The impression of life they give is purely visual and therefore incomplete. Some other factor has to be involved if it is to be completed.

The existence of this other factor was brought home with great effect many years ago. I was fishing, as a guest, at Broadlands at the time and suddenly saw a fish come at least ten yards to take the fly. It came over the top of a large, dense weed-bed on my side of the river with such a formidable bow-wave that it caught my eye although my attention was elsewhere at that moment. It made straight for the fly, took it and was hooked.

I told my host of this with some excitement when we forgathered for luncheon, imagining that I had seen something remarkable. To my surprise he was unimpressed. 'Oh we see that all the time,' he said. 'It's quite commonplace, but it *is* one of the things which makes fishing here so exciting!'

It was not until later that I began to wonder just how that fish had known the fly was there, observing that the weed-bed had been in the way when it had started off. It couldn't possibly have seen it, because the weed-bed was too big and dense. Nor could it have been the impact of the line hitting the water which had alerted it, because it was beyond belief that it could have connected that with the presence of a fly. There was no doubt at all about its being fully

93

aware of the latter's presence and precise position because it made a bee-line for it at high speed without hesitation. Of course it *might* have risen and, possibly, got a view of the fly over the top of the weed-bed, but the clear water over this was negligible, so that wasn't a satisfactory explanation either. Moreover my host had, over the years, often seen fish coming over the tops of weed-beds to be hooked, and he always fished the sunk fly at Broadlands (and worked it!).

My researches then showed that fish were perfectly capable of detecting the disturbances a fly makes in the water. The more obvious of these are its bow-wave and wake, which fish can detect by 'distant touch'. Another disturbance may also contribute to a fly's apparent life, and that is cavitation, which is always liable to occur with an imperfectly streamlined object over which water is passing.

Anyone can observe this phenomenon, if he wishes, by holding a fly by the cast in the fast water at the head of the pool. Then he will see what appears to be an air-bubble attached as a sort of tail to the downstream end of it. In fact this is not an air-bubble at all, but a pocket in the water in which there is a vacuum. This pocket appears to be relatively stable, but it is not. It is continuously collapsing and reforming at a very high rate and in so doing not only deceives the eye but also promulgates signals in a wide band of frequencies, usually referred to as 'noise'. A fish's aural equipment is ideally suited to receiving this noise and, as with other sound (and probably ultra-sound) emissions, the fish can home on it.

When selecting the reasonable fly, fishermen should, I believe, pay due attention to these factors, as already mentioned in Chapter 4. In the early spring and late autumn they will have no great difficulty in doing this because the large sunk fly is on a par with spinning baits and wobblers and is representing the type of creature they represent. The greater the disturbance it creates the better, because it could never make one quite as great as the baits. So in those times of year I believe it is advisable to employ large tube-flies or toshes, because their blunt ends create bigger disturbances than the more streamlined conventional spring/autumn fly would do. Their exact size is immaterial, so long as it is big, and the best dressing for them is the streamer-type which will further enhance it.

It is in the late spring and summer, when fishing with low-water patterns, that attention to the disturbance factors becomes much more important. If the fisherman concludes that a small fly is the reasonable one to use it may be that he should choose one which is double or treble hooked and chunky. On the other hand, if he decides on a large fly it might be advisable for him to choose a slimmer, single, hooked fly for fear of over-doing the disturbances and putting fish off.

In other words the impression of life the fly confers should always be natural, and for that reason he needs to take into account what the fly is likely to represent to the fish. When fished off a floating line this will almost certainly be a shrimp or an insect, and low-water flies fished sunk may represent these too. Indeed an entomologist once told me that my favourite fly, which I have used successfully off sunk and floating lines in many parts of the United Kingdom, is a very fair representation of a type of nymph when in moving water. I hope it is; Oliver Kyte's Agile Darter for instance; because that would provide a sensible reason for its general success and reinforce my belief that artificial flies should always represent, however sketchily, what fish will naturally expect to be present in their environment if the danger of putting them off is to be avoided.

The problem of deciding what is reasonable, from the point of view of the disturbances created, is not as difficult as it might seem, especially after plenty of opportunities to experiment. When the fisherman finds an appropriate answer to it, the dividends it pays can be impressive.

The other factors which point the way towards determining what is a reasonable fly for given conditions are much more straightforward. Dressing is important, as already discussed, and if the fisherman does not dress his own flies it will be to his advantage to find a fly-tier who really understands, and can give effect to, what is required.

Colour is important too, but it is quite unnecessary to be finnicky or fanciful about it. The fisher should bear in mind that ultimately the fly may come within the fish's visual range, and that sensitivity plus contrast determines how easily the fish will then see it. The fish provides the sensitivity, and it is up to the fisherman to select the fly which will provide the necessary contrast. That should not be too difficult for him.

Finally he has to make up his mind as to what would be a reasonable size, and this is very largely a matter of finding the right balance between hooking power and the danger of putting fish off. Rivers vary in this respect, because their characteristics are different. Indeed there are so many variables affecting reasonable size that it is impracticable to give more than one general rule about it.

This is that the fisherman in the late spring and summer should employ as large a fly as he dares when fish are taking freely, and only reduce the size when fish seem to be stiff or takers few. In this, only experience can guide him. Then, as soon as conditions improve or seem likely to improve, he should revert to the larger fly again with its better hooking power.

It is inevitable that individual fishermen, with the benefit of their individual experience, will come to their own conclusions about what is or is not the reasonable fly to suit the conditions. It is not something which lends itself to being specified within narrow limits, and the tolerances are considerable. Fish are not pattern and size connoisseurs, as they have sometimes been made out to be. There is no subtle colour shade or mystical micrometrical measurement which will, when others fail, induce them to take. When they are taking with a will, practically anything will serve the fisherman's purpose. It is when they are not, and are easily put off, that the reasonable fly really comes into its own. The foregoing should only be taken as one fisherman's view of how to select it. For him this has proved always to be adequately productive and, on occasions, extraordinarily so.

17

Hooking

Mr Wood was not alone in trying to improve hooking power. The problem is doubtless as old as the sport itself. You have only to look at the number of different hook patterns which were developed in the last couple of hundred years to know that our forefathers had as much trouble with it as we do now. In those days, good hooking was believed to be due as much to good hook design as anything else, and every fisherman had his own fads and preferences. Few of these patterns would be obtainable today, and if you were to ask a contemporary fly-fisherman which he particularly favoured he would probably wonder what you were on about. He relies on his favourite manufacturer, or his fly dresser, to provide him with hooks of a sound design, and his only worry is over quality and reliability. If the hook looks right, is made of fine wire and is not too soft or too brittle he is satisfied. The only decision he needs to make is whether to go for singles, doubles or trebles.

For thirty years now, doubles are what I have used most. 'Why not trebles?' you may ask, and I use these too for sunk-fly fishing. There is no getting away from the fact, however, that they are heavier than doubles and, above a certain size, this is a disadvantage when fishing the floating line, especially in a sluggish river. Indeed, in the larger sizes, doubles are also too heavy in some circumstances, but as I normally resort to singles when fishing very large low-water flies, this is no problem for me.

In the very small sizes I believe the treble has other disadvantages. To begin with it makes neat fly-dressing rather more difficult (except with tubes), but in the main I dislike small trebles because I think they lead to more losses. To hook securely with them I have found it necessary for two of the three tiny hooks to have got a hold. If you have hooked your fish in the scissors this is no problem; in fact all three hooks may have gone home and there is overkill, so to speak. But elsewhere it is just a matter of luck whether it is one hook or two, and one hook doesn't seem to be adequate. I think that must be the reason for the high proportion of losses because on the occasions when I do land a fish on a small treble it is usual to find that two of the hooks have gone home. That seems sufficiently conclusive evidence on that point.

The same thing can of course happen with a small double, but in its case the frequency with which both hooks get a hold is noticeably higher. This may be because its design, with its two hooks at an angle of about 60 degrees apart, gives it a better chance of doing so than that of the treble, of similar gape and bite, with its hooks at 120 degrees apart. Anyway I think the double hook is the better bet in very small sizes, and when fishing the floating line prefer it in all sizes up to the large ones.

So much for hooks. Now what about hooking techniques? As always, when setting out to evaluate current theories and practices, it is worthwhile taking a look at the environmental and physiological facts first.

A salmon in a river ventilates its gills by opening its mouth, taking in water, and then closing its mouth again so that it can force the water through its gill-rays and out by the openings hidden by the opercula. It is a continuous process, sometimes fast, sometimes slow, depending on the fish's oxygen demand.

It was this regular opening and closing of the fish's mouth which led me to wonder if anything could be deduced from it to improve reliability in hooking. For example, it is obviously advantageous to try to set the hook when the fish has its mouth completely closed, as there may then be less likelihood of pulling the fly away from it. So, theoretically, a good time to achieve good hooking is at the moment a fish takes, because it is only at that moment that one can be reasonably certain that its mouth will be closed on the fly. At any other time one could not be sure, and good hooking then would be just a matter of chance.

This seems to be an argument in favour of striking, and indeed it is pertinent that to strike like lightning is absolutely essential if a salmon is to be hooked on the dry fly. All those who fish the dry fly agree about that, and maintain that it is the difficulty of so doing with a long slack line in the streamy water of a salmon river which accounts for so many fish being missed.

I once, too, had a ghillie who invariably struck even when fishing the wet fly. He said he had done so all his life, and saw no reason to change. He fished with the rod held high and struck the moment he saw the line move. I was lucky enough to see him do it, as I had given him my rod while I had a rest and happened to be sitting watching him at the critical moment. I must confess that I never saw the line move, but he did, and struck the fish most convincingly. When he landed it I told him he was a genius, and he was suitably self-deprecating.

It is also an argument advanced in favour of the sunk-fly technique of just waiting for the fish to pull and then for the fisher to pull back. The theory there seems clear enough, but is it sound enough, I wonder? It would be if, in order to give the pull, the fish had to have its mouth closed on the fly, but unfortunately that is not necessarily so. However, as the fisherman has no means of judging the exact moment of the take, unless he is prepared to emulate the nymph fisher, it is the only practicable way for him to proceed.

Now how about Mr Wood's method, in which one gives a fish slack line and a certain amount of law before tightening on it? Again, this is a theoretically sound procedure *provided* that the fly ends up in the scissors the right way round. Then it doesn't matter a jot whether the fish has its mouth open or closed when you tighten, it will still be well hooked. The proviso is absolutely vital, however, and as it would never seem possible to ensure that the fly *was* the right way round, even if one was sufficiently skilful to be certain that it was in the scissors before one tightened, I am not as enthusiastic about the method as I might be. As I have described in a previous chapter, I employed it religiously for years without conspicuous success, never landing many more (on average) than about 50 per cent of the fish I encountered. Then, when I switched to using doubles, it did not seem to have any advantage at all as regards hooking fish in the scissors. That is precisely why I discarded it when using doubles off a floating line.

In any event, I am not at all sure that Mr Wood's reasoning was sound. He obviously envisaged fish rising vertically to take the fly as it passed overhead, concluding that by releasing line at that moment and allowing the current to act upon it, the fly would inevitably be pulled back into the scissors. I do not believe that fish take the fly at all in that manner, and if Mr Wood's premise was unsound it is possible that everything which depends on it is just a waste of time. But of course one cannot be sure.

Consider for a moment the physiological facts. The fish's vision is monocular, with each eye having its own conical field of view within which objects are observed. Its brain is organised accordingly. I have never heard of any experiments to determine whether the two cones ever touch, let alone overlap, and it may be that they never do, except possibly at quite a distance away from the fish. As the fish moves to take, it is probable, therefore, that as it does so its brain will be receiving close-range information from one eye or the other, and it could not take the fly effectively in any way other than by turning on it.

What is more, if the two cones do not touch or overlap immediately in front of the fish's nose, and it seems likely that they do not, the fish will inevitably lose sight of the fly altogether before it takes it. This means that if it is to be sure of the fly ending up in its mouth its body will have to be tangential to the fly's path at the critical moment. That is in fact what I saw when watching that Miramichi fish. It rose in a curve from the bottom and met the fly absolutely head-on.

This is a very different picture from that of a fish rising vertically to take a fly when this is overhead, and leads me to the conclusion that there are four distinctly different types of take. The fish either:

(1) meets the fly and, having got it in its mouth, turns upstream as it returns to the bottom,

or (2) follows the fly and does likewise,
or (3) meets the fly and, having got it in its mouth, turns downstream in a circle back to the bottom,
or (4) follows the fly and does likewise.

If it has done nothing else, this conclusion has given me a lot of fun with takers over the past two or three seasons because I have been trying my hand at identifying the type of take on each occasion. To begin with it seemed an absolutely hopeless task, and often enough it was quite impossible, but there were occasions when I had some success and was therefore encouraged to continue with it. The first of these occasions was when I was fishing a pool which had a distinct stream, that is a narrow band of faster water running through it, and as the river was at summer level I was expecting to encounter a taker, if I met one at all, in this stream or on the edge of it. In the event, the fly was taken well off the stream and I said (out loud, which is a bad habit I have got into from fishing alone so much), 'I wonder if that fish followed the fly before taking?' And sure enough, when I had landed it and could see, it had been hooked on the 'wrong' side of its jaw, confirming that it had in fact been following the fly.

After a while at this game I felt reasonably sure that I was getting better at it. There was no way of proving whether some of my guesses were right or wrong but I began to feel more confident, for example, in my ability to recognise whether the fish had turned upstream or downstream after taking, by the quality of the pull. There were occasions when this was so solid and satisfactory that it seemed certain the fish had turned downstream. Alternatively, there were the 'gentle' takes when, if one took into account the strength of the current, it seemed certain the fish had turned up. In comparatively quiet water, the evidence of an upstream turn was even clearer because the gentle take would be followed by the line going absolutely slack.

This was not just an amusing exercise, either, because it began to throw up interesting possibilities. The 'sample' is not yet large enough for authoritative conclusions to be based on it, but from what I have observed so far I believe that fish will, if possible, turn to meet the fly when they take it, in preference to following it. I base this on the fact that the majority of them have been hooked on the 'right' side of the jaw or, when hooked in the tongue or palate, have the eye of the fly pointing towards the 'right' side. When hooked in the jaw or scissors there can be no argument about that, but when hooked elsewhere the fly could, I suppose, have been pulled round during the playing period to give a false impression, but I don't think that happens very often. I believe that when the strain is released the eye of the fly will nearly always tend to revert towards the side from which it had been driven home, even when this was the 'wrong' side.

I deduce from this belief that for a fish to follow the fly, in order to take it, there must be a good reason. That the fly's approach had been screened from the fish by obstructions, for example, or that the fly had fallen short or too close for the fish to have had time in which to meet it. I fancy that when I have got more evidence I shall find that it is a phenomenon which occurs in some pools more than others, the position and nature of the lies in those pools being the influencing factor. If this turns out to be so, it may be that, in those pools, one ought to try to present the fly differently, in order to give fish a better chance to meet it, because hooking a fish on the 'wrong' side of the mouth is clearly something to be avoided if possible.

Another possibility may be emerging, too, namely that when the fly is moving at a good pace the fish will tend to turn downstream after taking it. Conversely, when the fly is moving slowly the fish will tend to turn upstream. This is just an impression at the moment but, if confirmed by further evidence, it may be a pointer towards obtaining better hooking by contriving always to fish the fly at a good pace. In my experience more fish which have taken gently become unstuck than those which have given me a good pull, so anything which might encourage a downstream turn after the take must be good.

These are all things the fisherman can bear in mind, and maybe find useful. Nothing is of much use if the fish are coming short, however – a phenomenon which he will discover occurs at least once in every season, if he fishes for long enough periods. At one time I had the notion that its appearance was connected with the tapering off of a run, and that the tail-enders were the culprits, but further experience has made me discard this idea. Even parr and brown trout seem to be affected, judging by the numbers which will foul-hook themselves during one of its appearances. Sea trout too, by day anyway. At its worst, when it can drive the fisherman practically insane with frustration, I have hooked fish in the chin, a nostril and, once, in the gill-cover (*what* a wild business playing that fish turned out to be!), indicating that the fish coming short is just nosing the fly or otherwise playing about with it and never takes it in its mouth at all. I have tried everything that anyone has ever advocated for successfully hooking fish which are coming short, and from bitter experience have concluded that nothing works. It is just a matter of gritting one's teeth and waiting for their behaviour to return to normal.

As for the problem of whether or not to strike when a fish takes, I have pondered this for many years. The Lore tells us not to strike, which is a point in favour of striking! I have an objection to it which is purely personal, however. To be effective, split-second reactions are involved, and a very high degree of concentration. This would be very tiring. I fish day in and day out for months on end, and need my fishing to be relaxing. Also I have a feeling that to fish with the rod held high, striking immediately the line was seen to move, might not after all lead to good hooking, because in all probability the pull of a bent rod would be insufficient to get a double hook properly home – at least a hook of the size I prefer to use most of the time.

So what I have continued to do is to employ Mr Wood's method of hooking, for better or for worse, when fishing with a floating line and a low-water single. When fishing with a double, or deeply sunk flies, I keep the rod point near the water with the rod pointing along the line, and hold the latter firmly. In this way I hope to get the fish to hook itself when its mouth is closed. This is well enough on the cards, because the period between the fish taking and the hook going home will be minimal. These methods have proved to be reasonably satisfactory and are, I reckon, the best I can employ.

I cannot leave the subject there without telling you what one ancient ghillie had to say on the subject of hooking. He told me that if he had learnt anything in his lifetime of salmon fishing it was that when fish were not taking properly there was no way of hooking them properly. On the other hand, when they *were* taking properly they would be hooked properly whatever anyone did, or didn't do.

I think he deserves the last word.

— 18 —
Strategy

Finding the taking salmon is largely a matter of good strategy and persistence. The value of persistence may be widely understood, but the tyro may wonder what on earth strategy has to do with fishing, expecially if he refers to a dictionary and finds it defined there, in brief, as 'generalship; the art of war'.

If, however, a salmon fisher does not take due account of the strategic factors, and exercise generalship in some degree, he is likely to be placing himself at an unnecessary disadvantage. This is particularly so if he has a lot of water to cover. After all, the effort he can expend is limited, and if he does not expend it to the best advantage he will not be as successful at the end of the day as he might have been. Often enough it is strategic rather than tactical expertise which makes an average fisherman into an above-average one. Nevertheless, strategy tends to be a neglected aspect of the salmon-fishing art, and many fishers pay far less attention to it than they do to tactics.

This may be because, hitherto, they have been able to rely on their ghillies for strategic advice, but that era is passing and ghillies of the right calibre are becoming rarer and rarer. If a ghillie happens to be no more than a fetch-and-carry merchant, with little knowledge other than where pools begin and end, the fisher will suffer. Moreover, in these days a rod may well find that no ghillie is available for him at all, and therefore be forced to rely on himself. This can be very off-putting if he is not suitably prepared for it.

Good intelligence, in the military sense, is an essential prerequisite to the formulation of good strategy, and a fisherman on his own needs a great deal of information before he can hope to make a good plan for each day. Some of this information should be in his mind's eye, unless he is a newcomer to the water; but some he will need to collect in advance and some must await his daily observations.

The information he should have in his mind's eye is to do with factors which are more or less constant. He should know the general characteristics of the pools he will be fishing – deep or shallow, glidey or streamy – and whether they are holding pools or those in which fish usually just rest. He should know how their productivity is likely to be affected by height of water, and whether this is of crucial or little importance.

On some rivers – the chalk-streams, for example – a gauge may be hard to find and water levels may be regarded as having little bearing on success. On others – many Scottish rivers – gauges abound and the reverse is the case. Apart from indicating which pools are worth fishing and which are not, it is probable that the height of the water in those rivers is a guide to where, in a pool in ply, most of its fish may be found.

For instance, some pools have an optimum height at which they fish best, with their occupants spread over all the lies, but when the water level falls below this the main body of fish may

105

more probably be found towards the neck of the pool than elsewhere. Conversely, when the water level is above the optimum, the main body of fish may prefer lies towards the tail. This is not axiomatic, but is cited merely as an example of the type of information which can be strategically useful. When it comes to fishing extremely long pools, it can be very useful indeed.

By the same token, the time of year can affect this particular issue. In some rivers fish tend to prefer deep, sluggish pools in the early part of the season when the water is very cold, forsaking them only as the season advances or the temperature rises. Again, in summer the streamy pools may be preferred to the glidey pools, and in high summer fewer fish may be found in the pools than in the runs.

A fisherman should, as I say, be thoroughly knowledgeable about all this as it applies to the particular water he will be fishing. If he is not, he should certainly make a point of becoming so, because it is pretty basic stuff. If he is coming to a water for the first time, it is therefore most desirable, if not positively essential, for him to have made a reconnaissance of it in advance, in the company of someone who knows it really well, and to have asked all the right questions. If he does that, noting down all the answers and not just trusting to memory, he will at least have made a good start.

One of the more important pieces of information the fisherman will need to collect (preferably before he starts his week or fortnight) is the distribution pattern of the fish. In some seasons, or parts of a season, they will favour certain pools or stretches of river more than others, and it is most important to have found that out, when it occurs. It may not be readily apparent to the eye, and in discovering it for himself the fisherman may waste good fishing time which could otherwise have been spent more profitably.

It is extremely useful, in the strategic context, to know that such-and-such a stretch is hardly worth fishing because fish will not now lie in it for some reason, and a prudent rod will ascertain these facts in advance and so save himself the trouble of doing it the hard way.

He should also find out what sport has been like recently. Quite a lot can be deduced from this. To begin with, it gives an indication as to the proportion of the fish population which is on the move, and this in its turn provides a weighting factor as to the relative importance of resting *vis-à-vis* holding lies. Moreover, if the number of fish moving is appreciable, he may also be able to determine, from the quality and pattern of the sport enjoyed, whether they have been passing through in concentrated groups, well spaced, or in a sparser, steadier trickle. This can affect the way in which he deploys his effort against them to the best effect, but many fishers never give it a thought.

Moreover, he should not seek this information just about his own water, but also as regards selected beats between it and the river mouth, because in that way he can get a preview, so to speak, of things to come. When sport is bad, and there is a natural tendency to relax effort, the ability to deduce, from information received from beats below, when it is likely to improve can be very useful in ensuring that good opportunities are not missed.

Then there are the time factors to be considered. The time of year is clearly relevant, as already mentioned, and some fishers attach great importance to the time of day. There is a lot of mumbo-jumbo attached to this, but it is certainly true that in some seasons or parts of a season there are periods when better sport is enjoyed in the forenoons than in the afternoons, or vice versa, as records show. This may be something of which due notice should be taken.

There are also two specific times in the day which require particular consideration – morning and evening twilight. Sometimes it will be worth expending a special effort on them, sometimes it will not. Again some fishers make a great to-do about this decision, invoking all sorts of mysterious and dubious influences, but the best basis on which to make it is whether or not fish are moving.

If they are, sport at these times can be very good. When a large number of fish are moving, it can be positively electrifying. On the other hand, when the fish population is more or less static, the twilight periods can be no better times in which to be fishing than any other. When that is so, it is probable that to fish the morning twilight period, in particular, is not worth the sacrifice entailed.

In order to give due weight to the time factors, a keen and active rod may therefore feel it necessary to split his day into four periods – morning, forenoon, afternoon and evening. At the beginning or end of a season it may be perfectly practicable for him to fish all four, but in the middle of the season obviously not. He has to sleep some time, and if he has been fishing up to midnight and then has to bag up his fish for dispatch next morning it will be 1 a.m. before he can get to bed. That will allow only two hours or so for sleep if the alarm has been set for fishing to be resumed at the onset of morning twilight, and clearly that is not a practicable routine unless some period for sleep is found during the day.

Consequently it is necessary for him to weigh up all the pros and

107

cons and decide on a realistic programme, so that he may not find himself too tired to continue to fish just when his chances of success are becoming good.

Finally, there is the information which has to be gathered by daily observation, because it can vary so much from day to day – the height of the water, temperatures, and weather conditions. The degree of importance to be attached to each depends largely on the personal convictions of individual fishermen. Some people are dominated by Fahrenheit or by the barometer, some are not, and the extent to which these factors are allowed to influence strategic decisions will vary accordingly. Certainly blazing sunshine can affect where fish are likely to be lying (especially in rivers lacking weed-beds to provide shade), as can wind or lack of it, and most people will give these things due weight. But, in general, the height of the water (except possibly in the chalk-streams) is the most important one, as already inferred, and will in consequence be the paramount influence.

Well, that is a survey of the principal strategic considerations and I hope it will not seem that to reach reasonable conclusions is too difficult or complicated. When a fisher gets used to the idea of having a specific strategy each day, it will become an automatic process, and whatever decision he reaches he will probably have a decisive advantage over the man who merely fishes aimlessly.

The sad thing about it all is that it is a dying art. Due to the pressure for fishing these days, more and more rods are being packed on to waters which should not properly be accommodating them, and the wretched fisherman thus suffers twice over – first, because the water is being overfished; second, because this largely denies him the pleasure of exercising his strategic expertise.

This trend is particularly noticeable when a rod is fishing at other than the 'best' times. In the old days it was recognised that a water which was adequate for a given number of rods in, say, the spring should not be expected to support more than half that number once the 'best time' was over. Nowadays, this sensible way of going about things tends to be thrown overboard, and water is often let on the basis that it can support the greater number throughout the season.

I can remember, when I was young, often finding myself the only rod on half a dozen miles of potentially good water and learning the hard way that without good strategy I would inevitably be wasting my opportunities. Nowadays, the chances are that I find myself on a beat with only two or three pools, all possibly out of order, with a consequent room for manoeuvre which is negligible.

Happily, though, it is not always that way.

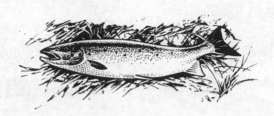

—— 19 ——
Luck

There is no doubt that, in life, some people are lucky and some are not. Napoleon was absolutely right about that. I dare say we all know of those who have only to buy a Premium Bond or two for the cheques to start rolling in as soon as their bonds become effective. On the other hand there are those who have purchased the maximum number and yet never win anything, even though they hold them for years.

In a sport like salmon fishing, where being in the right place at the right time can be a dominating influence in success, luck is sometimes bound to play a part. Years ago this was illustrated to perfection on the Aberdeenshire Dee.

Jack, who is a beautiful fisherman, had just fished the Whin Bush pool from the Kincardine side without success and had climbed up to the Kincardine hut to join his family and friends gathering there for luncheon. A few minutes later, along comes Bruce to fish the pool from the Carlogie side.

Now Bruce had been introduced to salmon fishing only some two or three days previously and his casting, as he would be the first to admit, was then still at the elementary stage. He started to fish employing the 'heap throw', which was his most effective cast at that time, and in due course a fish thrust its head up through the coils to seize the fly. Bruce, who was gazing around, taking in the beautiful scene with its fascinating flora and fauna, remained unaware of this. Indeed, as he told me afterwards, he believed that his prospects of interesting a fish were nil, and his main aim at that time was to get through the morning as quickly and painlessly as possible while waiting for the gin-pendant to be hoisted at the Carlogie hut.

Eventually, the fish made its presence felt and Bruce, to his great astonishment, found himself in business.

Before long, his line was round a rock, but again Bruce remained blissfully unaware of this, and played the rock with unabated enthusiasm until, after a while, the obliging fish got the line clear. Finally the fish was played out and had to be beached. Bruce achieved this by getting behind it and driving it ashore, and in the process looked just as though he was driving a governess-cart.

Full to overflowing with his achievement, he looked hopefully towards the Carlogie hut, but it still was not yet gin time and no one was about. Bruce therefore waded back in again to while away the remaining moments until it was, and there were.

In the meantime, Jack's family had been urging him to go down and fish the pool again, behind Bruce, and he had had some difficulty in convincing its members that there would be no point in this; that Bruce's success was just a flash in the pan and a typical example of beginner's luck.

I won't prolong the tale, although it is as full as an egg of incidents similar to those already recounted. Suffice it to say that Bruce got two more fish, one after the other, the last one in front of his admiring friends with gin and tonics in their hands. Gin time had at last arrived and Bruce, thankfully, called it a day.

The postscript is significant. Bruce's performance had, in the end, been too much for Jack, He seized his rod, went down to the pool and fished it a second time. Blank, like the first!

No doubt many fishermen will have similar incidents in mind which illustrate the part luck can play in success – isolated incidents, usually associated with beginners. But there are experienced fishers who seem invariably to be lucky and whose success rate is always above average. What of them?

From time to time I come across just such a man, of whom his colleagues tend to stand in awe. They will even attribute his success to his having some mysterious power with which he attracts fish to his fly. A gift rather like that possessed by a dowser, but in reverse. I cannot join them in this, as I am not one of those persuaded that in salmon fishing there are 'stranger things in heaven and earth, Horatio'. My philosophy is to look for basic causes.

When one studies such a man it invariably becomes apparent that he is one who pays the greatest possible attention to every conceivable detail. He will take infinite pains to get everything just right. Although no single thing he does is calculated to have more than a marginal effect on his fishing, it is the sum total of them all that makes its impact and accounts for his success. Preoccupation with his gear and tackle; care in presenting the fly exactly as it should be, and varying it to suit the time of year or prevailing conditions; never fishing aimlessly but always with due regard to the strategic factors; studying to be quiet both as regards noise and dress; appreciating when chances are likely to be good and ensuring that he spares no effort at such times; conserving his energy for that purpose; persisting when others might consider they have done enough; never allowing his sisters or his cousins or his aunts to parade up and down on a high bank in bright-coloured clothing (or at all!); likewise never doing anything, himself, which might distract a fish's attention from the fly; and so on and so on – the list is almost endless. These are the things which make him special, each little trifling detail adding to his chances although the contribution each makes is small. That is his secret, and not some mysterious 'fluence.

And it certainly isn't just luck!

20

Ghillies

The days when a gentleman never fished unless accompanied by a ghillie are vanishing like the snows of yesteryear. In the old days a ghillie was available for every rod, and it was the accepted practice that one employed him as a matter of course. Nowadays there may be just one ghillie for the entire water. In fact that is becoming the rule rather than the reverse.

Even lairds, nowadays, can be seen fishing unaccompanied, accepting that their ghillie has other more important things to do. Of the others, only first-timers on a water, the elderly, the infirm or the very rich now normally employ a personal helper and the sport has lost a lot in the process.

For the ordinary rod, it is not just the financial aspect which is the cause of this, but rather the growth of the nine-to-five outlook among ghillies which makes him so unwilling to employ one. He feels that a ghillie who starts fidgeting about at half past four in the afternoon, wanting to pack up, and who is unwilling to come out at night when he is needed most, is not a good investment. This is an understandable point of view, and one can sympathise with it, but it is a depressing one nevertheless. One of the particular pleasures of salmon fishing used to be the special relationship that tended to develop between a rod and his ghillie, and it is very sad to see it being blown away by the winds of change.

Although ghillies, as a whole, are becoming a vanishing species now that the 'one man, one ghillie' principle has, perforce, been abandoned, they are not likely to disappear altogether. Their function will have changed, however, and they will have become less of a helper and more of a supervisor. This, too, reflects the changing face of salmon fishing because there is no doubt that the increasing popularity of the sport has made supervision essential. More and more rods are appearing at the waterside who really do need supervising, and if there was no one to advise and control them all sorts of strange things might go on. Rules need to be interpreted to the uninitiated, and who could do this, in the field, if there was no ghillie?

I was fishing on a fly-only water the other day, for example, when a fisher appeared on the opposite bank with a spinning rod in his hand. He started casting, and I could hear the familiar plop close to my bank, so I walked back to the head of the pool and asked him if he had been told that only the fly was permitted on his water. He said he had, and was in fact fishing the fly. It transpired that he had not understood that the rule was intended to mean 'a fly fished off a fly rod'. There was no ghillie on his water or this misunderstanding would not have arisen.

Unfortunately it is not just the newcomers who need this sort of supervision, either. I have friends on one of Scotland's great rivers who are absolutely disgusted by the malpractices of some established fishers there, on waters where the supervision is lax or non-existent.

A ghillie also has an important role to play as the arbiter of good manners. He must not merely insist on his rods obeying the letter of the law in this respect but must also, by his own example, ensure that the spirit of it will be obeyed. Some ghillies seem no longer to appreciate this, or choose to disregard it, and some even actively encourage their rods to look upon the opposition as the enemy.

When two sides of a river are at loggerheads you may be sure that one or other ghillie is to blame. It is such a pity when this happens, because it must be quite obvious to all concerned that no one benefits, and that it makes fishing there unpleasant. Where, on the other hand, the relationship between the two sides is good, and everyone is at pains to ensure that no one suffers inconvenience or annoyance, fishing is the pleasure it always should be.

The first ghillie I got to know really well was the late Johnny MacIntyre, on Bonawe. When I knew him he was already an old man, but still strong and powerfully built. He was white-haired, blue-eyed, ruddy of face, and sported a magnificent white handlebar moustache. He took great pains with his appearance, and was always beautifully turned out. His tweed knickerbocker suit was immaculate, his brogues always shining. With his tweed hat on his head, and a gaff in his hand, he looked the epitome of what every Highland ghillie should be.

He was not the sort of man to let pride in his appearance stand in the way of efficiency, however, and nothing would prevent him from wading in to gaff my fish if he thought this desirable in order to ensure that I would not lose it. This used to bother me a lot, because I hated the idea of the old man spending the rest of the day in wet clothes, but nothing I could say or do would discourage him. I admired him tremendously and, in my innocence, thought that all ghillies would be like him. And most of those I had met up till then were, indeed, cast in the same sort of mould. When I went to the Aberdeenshire Dee, however, I found that there was another sort of ghillie. This was one who was not permanently employed by an estate, and housed, clothed and generally looked after by it, but was employed just for the 'season'. And this 'season' was short, being merely the four months from 1 February until 31 May. His wages were low, he did not have the advantage of free clothes or equipment, and there was no one to look after his interests but himself. Naturally his outlook was somewhat different.

This was brought home to me in a most salutary manner. I had hooked and played out a good fish, and had selected a shelving sandy bay in which to swing it in to be gaffed. The fish hung just out of reach of the ghillie for a moment and he remained immobile. I swung it in a second time, and exactly the same thing happened. The ghillie had merely to step forward with one foot into a couple of inches of water in order to gaff the fish, but he refrained. With my experience of Johnny MacIntyre in my mind, I thought that this was

115

quite extraordinary. However, I swung the fish in again a third time but still the ghillie did nothing. In my anxiety to get it within his reach I was too heavy-handed, the cast broke and the fish was 'awa'. With curiosity uppermost in my mind I said 'Why didn't you gaff it, George?' and he rounded on me with the words 'Some of you —— people would have us wade in up to our —— necks!' This wasn't a very good start to our relationship, but I'm glad to say that we soon became fast friends. He gave me an insight into the casual ghillie's point of view and I sympathised with it. Among other things, he told me that they all felt strongly that they should at least be provided with gum boots, or even thigh waders, when they were taken on, and that it was to put some force behind this that he had determined not to put even a toe in the water. I must say that this seemed perfectly reasonable to me, and still does. I have a high regard for a man who elects to take temporary employment as a ghillie from a love of the sport, even though he knows that, at the end of it, he will be out of work. The fringe benefits – a dram or two and a few tips – hardly make up for that.

Of course, there are all sorts of ghillies, some good, some bad, some whose ideas and advice are to be relied upon, and some whose counsels have their own interests in mind rather than yours. There is no doubt that many of them, especially the less experienced ones, have far too high a regard for the Lore. The myth that salmon will not take in the dark, for instance, was probably started and perpetuated by ghillies anxious to get home to their beds. Similarly, ghillies tend to propagate the fallacy that, in the early spring, salmon will not take early or late in the day, because they prefer that you do not start to fish before ten o'clock in the morning or continue after four in the afternoon at that very cold time of year. In actual fact early and late fishing may be just as productive in the early spring as it is at any other time. On one water I know of, it was the rule at one time that anyone who had the pool nearest the hotel should make a point of fishing it before breakfast, and many a good fish was taken from it at that time. Similarly, evening twilight can be a very good time then, and it is a great mistake to pack up too early.

One of my ghillies gave me an object lesson in the natural gamesmanship some of them possess, the first time he ghillied for me. He had started me off on a certain pool, but before I had got very far, called me ashore again. He then cut off my Thunder and Lightning, or whatever perfectly good fly it was that I had on, and substituted a fly of his own tying, saying that he thought it would be better. I then waded in again and a few minutes later hooked a fish, as he knew perfectly well that I might whatever fly I had on. As a result I became hooked on that particular fly of his, and it has remained one of my favourites ever since.

I have also noticed that, when the fishing is bad, his flies suddenly become unavailable in some mysterious way. On the other hand, when the fishing is good, he will be turning them out by the score.

Some ghillies tend to become absolutely hidebound in their views and resent it if you ignore these. I remember one occasion, when I was fishing as a guest and the river was unusually big. In consequence, a bay at the head of one of our pools, which at normal levels did not form part of the pool at all, looked rather promising. I saw my host looking at it speculatively, and eventually heard him ask the ghillie if it was worth fishing. The reply was that it was not. Later, my host decided to fish it anyway and, to cut a long story short, eight fish were taken out of it by the time we were due to return south. 'What do you think of it, now, George?' asked my host. 'Aach! It's no good!' the ghillie replied!

There are far fewer casual ghillies available in England than in Scotland. In the south of England the tendency for years has been to have just one river keeper for each water, long before a similar situation developed in Scotland. Often enough his duties differ from those of the Scottish ghillie too. Keepers now do more than just cutting and maintaining the banks, and generally looking after those fishing. On some waters the keeper has developed into a kind of business manager with his empire including trout-fishing and coarse-fishing offshoots. When these are large and important enough he may have assistants but they will be less concerned with actual fishing than with looking after hatcheries and stew-ponds under his supervision or in issuing day tickets. He will be accountable for the financial success of such enterprises and be a very important member of the estate's staff in consequence.

The old-fashioned ghillies of my youth were very preoccupied with tackle and would not let you fish with gear that they considered unsuitable. Many were the times that my tackle earned their pitying glances and was put aside in favour of their own. Johnny MacIntyre was an exception, thank goodness, because when I first went up to fish the Awe I was not very suitably equipped. He did not bat an eyelid, however, but merely did his best to help me to use what I had to best advantage. This was just as well, because I could never have accustomed myself to using his gear if I had tried for a month of

117

Sundays. I realised this on an occasion when he came down to the river one summer afternoon to get a fish for the house. Apart from being staggered by his success in doing so because conditions were so unfavourable, I was further rocked to my foundations by the equipment he was using. The rod was obviously older than he was and would be a prized collector's piece these days. I don't know what it was made of, lancewood I suppose, as it weighed at least twice as much as did my Forrest rod, although of comparable length. There was no new fangled nonsense about it, such as cork for the handle, or even a vellum covering; the handle was just of plain wood. The line was the heaviest I have ever seen, a huge cable in fact; but what really made my eyes pop out was the terminal tackle. The cast was barely 2 feet long and immensely thick. It was quite opaque and hairy with use and age. He told me that it was of Japanese gut-substitute, and, I would guess, of about 100 pounds breaking strain. The fly would have been more suitable, to my mind, for the spring, being a Green Highlander of a size round about 1/0. I was absolutely horrified by all this. I offered him casts – my beautiful Spanish gut casts – and any flies he liked from my well filled fly-box, but he would have none of them. I was not at my tactful best. 'Why not, Johnny?' I asked. 'How can you bear to fish with that – that – contraption?' As he had just taken a fish with it, and I had failed to do so for several days, despite an apparent advantage in casts and flies, my rudeness was quite unforgivable. But all he said was 'It suits me', and I felt very ashamed.

He then handed me the outfit. 'You try it!' he said. You can guess what happened. I did not actually tip up into the water but could easily have done so had his great hand not gripped my shoulder and prevented it. I need hardly tell you that the line and cast fell on the water in coils, almost at my feet.

He was a great companion, rather shy and quiet at first but eventually more forthcoming and confiding. I have had so few compliments paid me in my life that I prize them all, but the one Johnny paid me one day, in his artless fashion, I value most of all. He had been talking of all the various people for whom he had ghillied in the past, commenting on how few had seemed to realise that blank days were the rule in salmon fishing, rather than the exception, unless fishing at the 'best time'. He then said, out of the blue, 'I like fishing with you because you never complain!' I have never forgotten that remark, and have tried to live up to it ever since.

When fishing the Awe I used to stay at the Taynuilt Hotel, run by the Gunns. Most of the Awe fishers used to stay there and it was fascinating to sit in the bar of an evening and listen to their stories. On one occasion there was a well-known physician, from the south, staying in the hotel, who had the following story to tell.

On the previous day he had been fishing the Garravalt pool, with the bait, when he had hooked one of those monsters for which the Awe was famous. He had struggled with it for what seemed like hours when, to use his own words, the fish had decided that enough was enough and had headed for the sea. Off it had gone, with him running after it, until the bridge was reached. There the inevitable happened, the fish shot through the arch, the doctor's line ran out to a clinch, and he was broken.

Next morning he had again been spinning the Garravalt using his spare rod and, when he had reached the spot where he had hooked the monster the previous day, he had got snagged in something. He and his ghillie had done their best to get his bait free, and had discovered that it was foul of another line. Eventually they had got hold of this to find that it was in fact the doctor's broken line of the day before. Moreover, they found that the fish was still on. So the ghillie was sent off to get the other rod, which still had some of the broken line left on its reel, the two ends were joined together, and the doctor started to play the fish for the second time. Again he struggled with it for ages until, as before, the fish decided to 'head for the sea' with the doctor running after it. Eventually they reached the bridge, the fish shot under it, and the doctor was broken for the second time.

There is no doubt that the story was perfectly authentic and I thought it was a very remarkable happening. I told Johnny about it the next day. I expected him to be suitably impressed and waited with interest to hear what he would say. He said absolutely nothing at all. So I prodded him, verbally, but still he said nothing. By this time I realised that he didn't believe a word of it, and challenged him to say so. He asked who had been the ghillie, and when I had told him, wasn't reassured by that, either. 'Surely Johnny, you don't believe that Dr X would have made the whole thing up?' I asked him. There was a long pause, and then Johnny said cautiously, 'Wee-ll, it *might* be true!'

I suppose there were some aspects of the story which had caused him to mistrust it. First of all, fish very seldom 'head for the sea' unless they have been hooked by the tail, and this one clearly had not because the doctor had played it for quite a while, perfectly normally, before it had done so. Similarly, it must have seemed remarkable to him that a fish could have regained its original lie in the Garravalt, from a point somewhere below the bridge, with all that length of line streaming behind it. And I suppose he thought it likely, in the twenty-four hours intervening, that it would have rid itself of the hook somehow. Whatever his reasons were, the story obviously did not convince him.

More recently, I heard an even more remarkable story. Again there is no doubt about its authenticity and again, strangely enough, it was a well-known doctor who was involved. Someone fishing Lower Woodend had hooked a big fish with a spoon, and had clearly got it by the back. Eventually the trace broke and the fish was free. Some time later, the doctor was fishing the Three Stones pool on Lower Woodend, with the bait, when he, too, hooked a big fish by the back. It led him a hell of a dance, taking him down into Cairnton where eventually he managed to land it. In the process he thought there was something very strange going on because his bait, which was a minnow, seemed to have become transmuted into a spoon. When he got a better view he could see that one of the hooks of his triangle had actually entered the eye of the swivel of a spoon which, in its turn, was firmly hooked in the fish's back. The odds against such a thing happening must surely be of the order of billions to one.

I wonder what Johnny would have made of that story, if he had still been alive to hear it.

I cannot leave the subject of ghillies without recording how much I owe to them for their help and advice, especially in the early days. Much of my success then, such as it was, was due to their efforts, and from their company I have derived a great deal of pleasure ever since.

I salute them all.

21
Fly-Rod Odyssey

It was Negley Farson, I think, who wrote at length about his special feeling for fishing rods. As far as I can remember he called them his magic wands, because of their power to translate him to some of the most beautiful parts of the world. He compared his feeling for them to the love of a violinist for some fine instrument, and his joy in using them to the joy of a musician when playing soul-stirring music. He took them with him wherever he went, not merely for use but also because of their association with happy times and valued friendships. He spoke of their ability, just by being there, to lift his spirits when they were low and said that he could never feel lonely when he had them with him.

I suppose that most of us feel much the same way about ours.

My rod cupboard is so biographical that when I open it and look at its inmates hanging there, in their rows, it is as though I am regarding my past in microcosm. Most of the rods I have ever used are there because I have never willingly parted with any of them, and when circumstances have sometimes compelled me to sell one I have always bitterly regretted it later. It is strange how this is so, because, apart from two or three, they hang there unused. But they are old friends and I suppose I value them accordingly.

The first salmon fly-rods I ever owned are not there, I'm sorry to say. In those days greenheart was U and cane non-U, and mine were all built of greenheart. One, I remember, was made by Forrest of Kelso. It was 16 feet long and ferruled. The Awe and all that Spey-casting finished it off. Then there was one by Enright of Castleconnel, also about 16 feet long, which was a superb Spey-casting rod, and I like to think of it as lost at sea because it disappeared just after the war when I was serving in the Home Fleet.

To replace it I decided to treat myself to a Grant Vibration rod and

121

visited Playfair's shop in Aberdeen for that purpose. I shall never forget that visit because of the impression the shop left on me. No doubt the years have distorted it, and the shop was never quite as I remember, but in my mind's eye the light was dim and the place had a distinctly ecclesiastical air about it, with a wonderful smell of wood and varnish, like incense.

Adding to this impression was the bespectacled, apron-clad figure standing behind the stark counter rather like a priest at the altar, and the whole place gave me the same sort of feeling I get when visiting Westminster Abbey.

I made my business known and was shown some beautiful rods; then a huge leather-bound ledger was produced in which my order was to be recorded. This read like a cross between Burke's Peerage and the Almanac de Gotha. The names of kings, grand-dukes, princelings, ambassadors and practically everyone of note seemed to be written there in copperplate script but, alas, mine was not to be added to them. After much scratching of the head, and complicated calculations, I was told that my order could not be filled for at least two years, and that was no good to me. So I did not place it. Instead, I bought a couple of Grant Vibration rods second-hand, one from a Spey angler who had decided to change to cane, and another, shorter, one from a Dee angler. The first one was 15 feet long and I still have it. The second was a 12-footer which I swapped for an Enright rod of the same length, and I still have that. I believe that the man who took the Grant rod in exchange still has it too, but I'm not sure. All three are, or were, marvellous rods.

It was probably just as well for me that Playfair's shop had such a backlog of orders because, after the war, good, seasoned greenheart rapidly became unobtainable. Playfair's eventually went out of business because of this, and also because the craftsmen who had carved the greenheart were, by that time, old men who were dying off. But my 15-footer was a rod of pre-war vintage, in first-class condition, and I continued to use it for several years. Unlike the Enright rod it never broke and it was only because of its length and weight that I eventually pensioned it off.

I eventually pensioned off the Enright rod, too. Twice the butt broke on me and, for its replacement, a new butt had to be made from scrap, because new greenheart was then such rubbish. The repairs were never quite successful and, indeed, good-quality greenheart rods which had been scrapped became quite difficult to find. So the change to a cane rod became inevitable.

By that time I was an ardent disciple of Mr Wood and was embarked on a dalliance, which turned out to be lengthy, with short rods. I must have been crazy, but I got the idea firmly in my head that Mr Wood's great success was largely due to his fishing single-handed, and I decided to do likewise. I knew I could never handle a 12-foot rod in that way, as Mr Wood had done, but when I was in the States an American friend had lent me an 11 foot single-handed Leonard rod to try, which I had liked, so I thought that I would make do with a rod of similar length to that. I was an innocent, in those days, and had no idea that Leonard rods were something special.

So, one day, I went into the London shop of a famous rod maker and told the assistant, who had looked after my tackle requirements since I was a boy, exactly what I wanted. I thought he looked at me rather strangely, and seemed to hesitate a bit, but in the end he said that the rod would have to be made to special order, as none of their standard rods would fill the bill. He said that, just to make sure, he would have the rod sent down from the factory 'in the rough', so that I could see what it would be like when finished. And off I went, rejoicing.

Two or three weeks later he rang up to say that the rough rod had arrived, so I rushed round, full of the joys of spring, to inspect it. He placed it in my hand without a word. It felt as though it weighed a ton! I looked at him in dismay and humbly asked him what he thought of it. 'It's a brute!' he said 'I'm going to send it back and tell them you won't have it.'

We then had a long discussion, during which my matchstick-proportioned wrists were inspected, but I still hankered after single-handed rods and eventually purchased a Viscount Grey. This was a simply beautiful fishing rod, but even so my wrists were not up to fishing it single-handed. After trying to do this on one or two occasions I had a butt extension made, which turned it into a lovely little double-handed 11-foot rod, and reluctantly discarded my ideas of fishing single-handed because I realised I just did not possess the right physique. Later the Viscount Grey was joined by other 11-foot double-handed rods.

Having fished with these short rods for a number of years, in the heyday of the greased line, I began to see that Mr Wood's methods were not all they were cracked up to be and I felt the need for longer rods. Also I had missed the feel and pleasure imparted by spliced rods and longed to get back to them. For a while I returned to my 12-foot Enright but, when that broke yet again, I realised that I must find some other rod, preferably of cane, which suited me. That was how I came to meet Chris Eggington, who had the reputation of being the best rod builder in the country at that time, and moreover was a builder of spliced cane rods.

With one exception, he is the last real craftsman with whom I have come into contact. He made his rods from scratch. I took my Enright rod to him and explained that I wanted to replace it with a 12-foot spliced cane rod of similar characteristics. We then went out to a shed, in the bottom of his garden, which was filled to the roof with whole cane. We spent some time in selecting appropriate lengths of this, or rather he did because I was not knowledgeable about cane, and then he took me upstairs to his workshop where he showed me how it would be tempered, split and transformed into blanks. At that time he worked quite alone, so when in the end he handed over the finished article he could say, quite truthfully, 'Built entirely by my own hand.'

From then on I went to him for years. During that time he made three spliced cane rods for me which were sweet and joyful to use. In addition I used to take all my rods to him for overhaul at the end of each season, and he would take great trouble over them, returning them to me as new. Almost too much trouble, in fact.

Few people realise how difficult it is to judge rods if one is not an expert, even when able to fish with them. Greenheart and cane can become tired, and eventually rods become clapped out without one noticing what is going on. But Chris was an expert, and had only to take a rod in his hands to tell you all about it. He could discern, unerringly, its shortcomings, and where it was deteriorating, and would rectify this on his own initiative. I didn't dare object to this, or say that I had found nothing wrong with the rod, because he was something of a prima-donna and temperamental, and I did not wish to risk giving him offence. Often, on receiving back my rods at the beginning of a new season, I would find that he had put whippings on here and there to improve their action, or had split and re-glued sections for the same reason. The former gave the impression to the uninitiated of breakages, and I was sensitive about that. The latter could be expensive and in those days, for one reason or another, I was often very short of cash. Nevertheless I swallowed my objections and we remained fast friends until, when well over eighty, he decided to give up and retire.

One afternoon, before this happened, we were sitting round the stove in the room behind his shop, and I told him the story about the

11-foot Leonard and how I had tried to obtain an equivalent rod in England but had failed. This amused him a lot because, he told me, he had gone over to the States to work for Leonard for a while in order to discover the secret of making such beautiful rods. He said that there was a secret all right, but that old man Leonard was far too astute to allow anyone to discover more than just that. According to Chris, Leonard was able to produce rods of comparable power, but with finer scantlings than anyone else, because of the glue he used. With this glue he could produce top joints, in particular, which were very much thinner and lighter than any we were able to produce in England, without surrendering any of their steeliness. In consequence of this, his rods were not only lighter, overall, than others, but also much better balanced and less heavy on the hand. The formula for this glue was something Leonard kept entirely to himself, so no one ever discovered the secret of it.

I was working in an offshoot of the National Physical Laboratory at Teddington at the time and, when corresponding with Sharpes of Aberdeen about a trout rod that I wanted, remembered what Chris had said about the importance of glues. So I mentioned, in one of my letters to Sharpes, that I knew that the development of extra-special waterproof synthetic glues had been proceeding apace as a result of war experience, and asked if the firm had ever considered them in relation to the possible development of spliced cane rods. At that time, the holding factor in this was the difficulty in maintaining the integrity of the splice, which tended to open out in use when conventional glues were used. Chris, at that time, always bound his splices with fine twine in order to prevent this. These had to be greased in order to permit them to work against one another in the proper fashion which was rather a nuisance and was the only thing I had against his rods. I never received an answer, but a few years later Sharpes produced their well-known range of spliced cane rods, and I have often wondered if my letter had anything to do with that. I like to think that it had.

Anyway, when Chris Eggington finally gave up, I turned to Sharpes when I needed a new rod, and found this new range absolutely splendid.

I was particularly impressed by the light weight and good balance of the 14-foot rod, and in using it realised how misguided I had been in thinking that short rods were best. In the final analysis there are so many benefits to be derived from length. Less effort is required in casting, despite the added weight. One just has to swing the rod back and forth and it does all the rest. With shorter rods there is always a tendency to add a bit of punch in order to get out line properly, especially when there is wind, as there usually is, and this isn't really a very good thing. Also, in fishing out the cast, a long rod gives better control. Playing fish is made much easier, too, because more line can be kept clear of the water and there is less danger of the line becoming drowned. Even my American friends, predisposed as they undoubtedly are to employing short rods, agree with all this as regards major rivers.

There is a happy mean, however, and I am not at all in favour of the tendency towards very long rods which is now manifesting itself. Apart from the difficulties of transporting such a long rod on a car, say, when 'up', they increase immensely the difficulty of bringing fish to the tailer or gaff unless one is fishing with a ghillie. As, nowadays, most of us do not, it is just as well to leave very long rods alone. Fifteen or sixteen feet is quite long enough for all practical purposes. To buy one longer than that is to let oneself in for a great deal of trouble.

Fibreglass, as a material for rod making is something I know little about, as I was put off it right from the start. I had a conviction that splices were essential in obtaining a sweet action, and were certainly the safest form of joint for Spey-casting, but these were not the only reasons. I am always interested in anything new to do with fishing, and a trial of these new glass rods was something I determined to have. My chance came when, not all that long after they first came on the market, I was fishing in Alaska. My American hosts had several and asked me if I would like to try them, which I did. They didn't think much of them, themselves, and I didn't either. Of course this is unfair comment because, at that time, not much was known about the new material and those early rods made from it were pretty nasty. They vibrated like well-struck gongs, and this would put anyone off. It was not until the manufacturers realised the importance of damping, and were able to modify their processes accordingly, that fibreglass rods became pleasant to use. One or two that I have tried in the past five years have been quite beautiful, and with the quality of cane deteriorating (or so it seemed) I was tempted to change to them. And I probably would have, eventually, had it not been for the development of carbon fibre.

As happened with fibreglass, the advent of this new material resulted in a crop of bad rods appearing on the market. Most of my friends rushed to buy them because, when one reaches a certain age, a rod of such lightness has a tremendous attraction. Conservation of one's energy has become a major problem, especially in the long days of mid-summer, and elderly backs have to be cosseted, if not corseted, if one is to get through the days without discomfort. But it seemed a peculiarity of the new material that, while it appeared perfectly satisfactory for trout rods, it was clearly unreliable when used for longer rods, and breakages abounded. Extraordinary, this, observing how much experience had been gained in the use of synthetic materials for rod blanks in the fibreglass era. I suppose it was that every rod builder wanted to be the first in the market with his products. It was a great pity, for whatever reason, because it must have put a lot of people off carbon fibre, and probably still does. It is not funny, if one has invested hundreds of pounds in purchasing a carbon-fibre rod, and got used to it, to have it break without reason and be forced to revert to glass or cane. I know, because that happened to me, despite delaying my purchase of a carbon-fibre rod until I reckoned all the bugs were out.

Apart from financial considerations, the change to carbon fibre is not one to be undertaken lightly especially if, as with me, the change is from cane. For the first fortnight or so I couldn't get on with the new rod at all, and very nearly reached the stage when I determined to send it back. Then things began to click into place and I began to like the rod very much indeed. Now, I wouldn't change it for anything. But I did break it in the process. It has spigot joints and, if the greatest care has not been taken with the materials of which these are constructed or in the way they have been reinforced, they are clearly a weak point, because of the sudden reduction in diameter from the blank to the spigot, which throws a great strain on the latter, and also because the walls of the blanks into which the spigot fits are so thin. Not only that, but the fit needs to be perfect otherwise, in casting, the blank tends to work up the spigot, unnoticed, increasing the strain on both. Anyway that is precisely what happened to me. I noticed what was happening, and did all I could to keep an eye on it, but I hooked a fish one day when the joint must have been loose with the result that the spigot, in this instance, broke. It could equally well have been the wall of the blank which had split.

Being forced back to my Sharpe rod was another shock. For a short while I couldn't cast with it at all, despite my long association with it over the years.

But to return to joints, I realise that the spigot joint is infinitely preferable to ferruled joints but nevertheless it is fundamentally mechanically unsound. From now on it will be a permanent worry for me, and I shall have to keep a candle on hand, constantly, to rectify the apparent impossibility of obtaining a proper press fit with these joints. If a rod builder really wants to be first in the field with his rods, I suggest he puts his mind to the production of carbon-fibre rods with spliced joints. It surely cannot be all that difficult to do. Imagine what a stampede there would be to buy them!

22

Tactics

Before discussing tactics proper, there are one or two things to be said about lines. These are tactical weapons, and as choice is involved it is necessary to comment on them first.

In case there may be some confusion in the minds of some fishermen about it, let me start by saying that it is perfectly valid to employ a sinking line at any time. Indeed, there are still a few fishermen who, despite Mr Wood, fish the sinking line throughout the season. In the early spring, when the water is very cold, it should in any case be preferred to the floating line for the reasons given in Chapter 6.

At other times in the season there is no evidence to prove that the one method is superior to the other as regards productivity, although there is prejudice about that, both ways. There is a possibility, however, that when water temperatures become very high the sunk line should again be preferred.

The floating line, which characterises the method which is so much the pleasanter and more popular of the two, should only be employed when conditions are right for it. As spring advances, and water temperatures become generally higher, the fisherman may select it if he wishes, but should be guided by Mr Wood's experience and only do so if air temperatures are higher than those of the water. In summer conditions, when water temperatures are higher still, it is doubtful, to say the least, if Mr Wood's restrictive dictum still applies and in my opinion fishermen need no longer pay any great attention to it.

A good rule for any fisherman who, like myself, does not wish to be bothered by taking temperatures or chopping and changing from one line to the other is, I suggest, to employ the sunk line in the spring or autumn and the floating line in the summer. He can then, I believe (unless the water temperature is abnormally high), be confident that he is fishing effectively and, moreover, be doing so with the minimum of bother.

At one time there was a belief in some quarters that bigger fish were killed with the sunk line than with the floating line, but the latter has now accounted for so many specimen fish that I'm sure that belief can no longer be justified.

Another point about lines is their colour. For sunk-line fishing it is usual to employ a dark line, and there is no controversy about that. As regards the floating line, however, opinion is divided. Some fishermen continue to favour dark lines for floating-line fishing while others, the majority perhaps, prefer those which are light-coloured or white.

The arguments in favour of white lines are, first, that they are easily seen by the fishermen at all times and accordingly help him in fishing the water effectively; second that they are less obvious to the fish because, being floating lines, it will only see them against the sky with which they will contrast less than would a dark line.

The first argument is valid enough but the second is suspect. It is true that a line floating on top of the water will not be seen by the fish until it enters the scope of the fish's window. Even so the fish would then be viewing the shady underside of the line which must inevitably appear darker than the sky and so be perfectly noticeable. Another fallacy of the argument is the fact that floating lines do not always float on top of the water. Even when perfectly clean and brand-new they will show beneath the surface in ripply, oily or broken water. The moment they do they will be viewed by the fish against any background, however ill defined, reflected by the underside of the water surface, namely the bottom or sides of the pool. On occasion this could be the situation for the greater part of the fishing-out process, and a white line would then be so noticeable that it might distract the fish's attention from the fly. As I attach great importance to avoiding that as far as possible, it is one of my reasons for disliking white lines. It seems too much of a price to pay for the doubtful advantage of seeing them better while fishing out the cast.

It is debatable, too, whether fish are put off at all by viewing dark lines against the sky, as we have been led to believe. In my experience salmon are not normally line-shy, and when they are the mere impact of the line falling on the water is sufficient to make them take off. When they are like that, the line could be any colour in the rainbow and it still would not make any difference.

One final point about the choice of tactical weapons is that they need to be suitable for the job in hand. Heavier casts are desirable when ice or grue is liable to be encountered; also at night or when the river is in flood. At night the fisherman may be unable to see what is going on well enough to avoid having to use strong-arm tactics, and in heavy water may have them forced upon him.

Similarly it is only sensible to employ, at night or in heavy water, flies which are going to take a good hold. Fish sometimes do very strange things in the dark, making long downstream runs for example, and if the fisherman is unable to follow because he cannot see well enough, or for other reasons, he may be forced to resort to very strange things himself. That is the only valid reason for employing big flies at night, because fish are perfectly well able to detect even the smallest flies in the darkest conditions through the disturbances they create.

Tactics, by definition, are skilful devices or procedures, calculated to gain some end, employed when in actual contact with the adversary. Many of particular interest have already been covered in other chapters, but a little more remains to be said.

When wading a well stocked pool in a wide river, the fisherman is faced with the question 'How far in shall I go in order to obtain the maximum tactical advantage?' In answering it he would do well to think in terms of 'his' fish and the opposition's. His fish are those he can cover easily at an appropriate angle; the opposition's are those which he cannot. Sometimes he can safely decide to strive to cover the opposition's fish, but he should avoid doing this if it in any way entails jeopardising his chances with his own. He should bear in mind that the possibility of hooking one of his own fish is far greater than that of hooking one of the opposition's, and may be quite good if he doesn't spoil everything. Nothing is more ludicrous than the spectacle of two fishers, on either side of a pool, each wading in as far as he can, disturbing his own fish in the process, in order to cast as far as he can into the other's water. A more sensible tactic is for each to concentrate on those fish which will give him his best chance of success. If this can be done with a short line, so much the better, because to fish a longer line than is absolutely necessary has many disadvantages and is best avoided. The optimum wading path is therefore one which will enable the fisherman to cover his own fish adequately, at the optimum angle, without having to pass too close to any of them. If he gets too close, fish will move away as he wades past them, and this may spook others which he has yet to cover.

Speed over the ground is something to aim for, as has already been pointed out. The fisherman may dwell for a while, by all means, to ensure that he has thoroughly explored the possibilities of known taking lies of particular importance. Some experienced fishers concentrate on them almost to the exclusion of everywhere else, because they believe this to be good tactics, and when fishing in the evening twilight it often is. At other times, when the possibility of their being tenanted is less, it may not be so good, and it is possible to waste a lot of time on them which could be better spent elsewhere. As a general rule, and good common sense, it is better just to give them every chance of yielding a fish and, if they do not do so quite quickly, to move on.

Many fishermen never realise how easy it is to distract a fish's attention from the fly by some unguarded act. Paradoxically it is easier to do this when fishing from the bank than when wading, because salmon are far less cautious about anything in their own element than they are of things outside it, so it is sometimes good tactics to wade even if it is impossible to get more than a few feet from the bank.

It is easy, too, to put them off taking the fly, when otherwise quite ready to take it. The fly's natural progress through the lies should not be interrupted by, for example, mending the line drastically. Nothing is calculated to put off a taking fish more effectively than for the fly suddenly to stop fishing and sink.

In most circumstances it is also desirable to fish out each cast to the bitter end and leave the fly at the dangle for two or three seconds in order to give any fish which may have been following it a proper opportunity to take it.

After making a cast, something well worth doing is to pull in, smartly, a couple of feet or so of line as soon as it hits the water. This is not only a means of getting the fly to fish with the minimum delay but also immediately rivets the attention of fish on it, both visually and through their other senses. It also enables the options to be kept open when a fish takes, because it will have provided the fisherman with slack line in hand, which he can then yield or hold as he thinks fit.

The problem as to what tactics are best employed after rising a fish is also an interesting one. Now that fly size is no longer regarded as being such a crucial feature of salmon fishing as it used to be, the old ploy of trying a fly a size or two smaller than the one the fish rose to, but did not touch, has fallen into disrepute. And rightly so, because it is reasonably certain that it is to the delay in presenting the new fly, rather than its smaller size, that success, if any, should have been attributed. And often enough it didn't succeed, possibly because the delay had not been long enough. Nowadays it is considered that a minimum delay of from ten to fifteen minutes is desirable in order to give a reasonable chance of success, and that one of up to two hours, or even more, will still produce the goods. By day at all events. At night the period during which a fish remains in a taking mood seems to be much shorter.

Waiting has its disadvantages, especially if there is the opposition to be considered. A rod on the opposite bank can hardly be expected to be pleased, if he is following his opposite number down a pool or waiting to get in, to see him hanging about, doing nothing, for ten minutes or so. Moreover, if there is no opposition to worry about it is a tedious and time-wasting business anyway.

So the tactics I now employ by day are slightly different. I continue to fish down the pool after rising the fish, but mark where my feet were when the fish was risen, and note the amount of line I had out. I then return to the spot later, pay out line to the mark, and make a single cast. When it works, as it frequently does, it seems like magic to anyone looking on, especially if he was not there when the fish was originally risen. It does wonders for one's reputation! Only when this merely produces another rise is it desirable to change the fly, and then factors other than the size of the fly should be taken into consideration. It may not have been size that put the fish off.

My main difficulty in employing this tactic successfully when wading is to identify the exact spot where I was originally standing. The precise length of line, on the other hand, is of no problem to me because I have my line marked by a whipping to indicate when there is a good fishing length out. But the exact spot from which I made the significant cast is often difficult to find when it is in the water, and in addition to taking cross bearings by eye, so to speak, in order to give me its approximate position, I now keep a couple of suitable markers in my pocket, and drop one.

A similar situation, needing appropriate treatment, occurs when a series of minute plucks have been felt when fishing down a pool, without there having been any visual indication of rises. There is no need to go to all the bother of marking the positions, and lengths of line out, in this instance. Just go back and fish the pool down again about an hour later. It is remarkable how often it will then be found that some of the plucks have been translated into takes.

So much for the skilful devices and procedures, insofar as they occur to me. The reader will have others in mind, no doubt, because rivers differ one from another and some demand tactics of a specialised kind. On the Cassley, to take just one example, 'backing up' is a favoured method of fishing some pools, and on some rivers it is necessary to work the fly, or even grease the cast (to cause the fly to skate), in order to stand the best chance of interesting fish. The main thing is to employ them all with confidence, as confidence breeds success. It is also desirable to cultivate the right attitude of mind, because this is as important as any tactical consideration. If the fisherman is one of those who imagine they can, by some particular skill, induce fish to take, then I'm sure he will be starting off on the wrong foot. It is a pretty conceit but one which, in my experience, is best discarded. Instead, he should remind himself repeatedly that his aim should be to find fish which happen to be disposed to take, and act accordingly. This is a much more sensible attitude to adopt and, I have found, a much more productive one.

23

The Hydrodynamics of
Playing Fish on the Fly

Hooked fish are contrary creatures. If the fisherman tries to bring them up in the water they will strive to stay down. If he tries to force them towards him they will fight to move away. This makes playing fish rather like a game of chess, where each move in the opening gambit provokes a response which is more or less standard and can be anticipated.

If the fish is small, its efforts to do these things will be comparatively ineffective and short-lived, so the fisherman can make mistakes and usually get away with them. With big fish it is quite a different matter. They are in a class by themselves. To get one of them under control may take a long time, and every mistake the fisherman makes will prolong the battle and increase the odds on the fish winning it. This chapter is therefore principally concerned with avoiding mistakes when playing big fish on the fly, and especially when playing them in wide, fast rivers like the Spey, the Aberdeenshire Dee and many Scandinavian waters. Avoiding mistakes, where practicable, very largely boils down to an understanding of the hydrodynamics involved, so here are some examples which illustrate the effect of these forces on a fly-line and consequently on the fish.

As the first example, assume that a fly-fisherman is playing a fish in a narrow canal. No wading is involved and he has complete mobility from start to finish because the banks are clear. There is no current to complicate things, and no rocks, weed-beds or other hazards to worry about. The canal is narrow, so he will not have any difficulty in keeping his rod point directly over the fish, or as near to that as makes no matter, and the line will be a reasonably accurate indicator of the fish's position at all times.

His aim from the moment of hooking should be to take up and maintain a position abreast of the fish from which he can exert the maximum practicable strain on it in a direction which is more or less vertical. The fish will respond to this by fighting to remain near the bottom. It may circle, or move up (or down) the canal, but this will pose no problems for the fisher because he can easily counter any move the fish makes by moving correspondingly so as to maintain the vertical strain. Eventually the fish will tire and become unable to resist the vertical pull any longer. The fisherman will then be able to bring it up to the surface and keep it there until it gives up and turns on its side.

That illustrates the art of playing fish in its simplest form.

Now imagine that there is a 5-knot current flowing in this same narrow canal and consider the implications of that. The modern salmon fly-line is comparatively bulky, especially if it is a floating one, and a 5-knot current will exert considerable force on it. Hydrodynamics have entered into the problem.

Because of this there will now be quite a pronounced curve in the line between the water's surface and the fish, and the fisherman cannot rely on the line any more to tell him precisely where the fish is, in all circumstances. Moreover, if his feet are more or less abreast of the fish, the pull of the line on it will no longer be purely a vertical one but will have a substantial downstream component. The fish will have this to fight against, in addition to fighting to stay near the bottom, and may respond, if it is powerful enough, by forcing its way upstream. If it does this, the fisherman may not be able to detect it at once, from observing the line, but the indications that it is in fact happening will be an increase in the strain on the rod and a hissing sound from the line where it cuts the water. If he knows what he is about he will then move upstream in double quick time until the hissing stops and the strain returns to normal. What he has done is to remove the downstream component of the pull and leave only the vertical component. The fish may now cease to continue its upstream run, but whatever it does he will, as before, counter any move it makes by moving accordingly. In doing this he should always aim to achieve the position, somewhat upstream of it, where only a vertical pull is exerted.

In due course the fish will again yield to the vertical pull and begin to come up in the water. The more it does so, the less will be the hydrodynamic influence on the line. When, in the end, most of the line is out of the water the fisherman can forget about hydro-dynamics and take up any position he thinks fit. The final stages of the battle will again have been reached.

If the fisherman does not move upstream smartly when the line starts to hiss, the downstream component of the pull on the fish will become paramount, urging it to fight its way upstream with all the vigour it possesses, and his line will become drowned. To retrieve *that* situation he will need to run upstream as fast as he can, hoping to undrown the line before the cast breaks or the hook pulls out. Better late than never!

That introduces another very important hydrodynamical point, which is best illustrated as follows. Imagine that our fisherman, on hooking it, moves upstream to a position which is virtually directly upstream of the fish, lying immobile on or near the bottom, and consider what would then result. The pressure of the current on the bight of the line will be to lift it upwards and hold most of it near the surface of the water. Conversely, if he assumes a position virtually directly downstream of the fish, the action of the current will be to press the bight down towards the bottom and hold it there, resulting in the line becoming totally drowned.

These are the two extreme cases, but if the fisherman takes up any intermediate position the difference will be only in degree. In other words, when a fisherman playing a fish positions himself anywhere upstream of it the tendency will be for the line to be lifted in the water and kept out of danger. When he allows himself to be anywhere downstream of his fish the pressure of the water will tend to press the line down towards the bottom and into danger.

It also illustrates clearly enough another point. Although a fisherman may be directly upstream of his fish, the fish may not necessarily be feeling a pull from that direction. By being easy on it the fisherman may substitute a downstream pull for the upstream one. It is possibly for this reason that the 'conning' tactic described in chapter 12 can often be so successful when the fisherman hooks a fish lying well below him.

Now imagine that our canal, complete with the current we have introduced, has become as wide as a major river. The fish's freedom of movement will not now be confined to one which is only up or down the water, with it always remaining more or less within reach of the rod tip, but will have had another dimension added to it. Consequently the fisherman will now be unable to take up any position from which to exert only a vertical pull. All he can do is remove the upstream/downstream component, but not the lateral one pulling the fish towards his own bank. This means that, in addition to fighting to stay down near the bottom, the standard response of the fish will be to fight its way towards the opposite bank. The more it does so the greater will be the danger, because more and more line will get into the water. When that happens the hydrodynamic forces on it will become more pronounced and, unless the fisherman does something about the situation, the danger of drowning the line will reappear.

This illustrates the point that it is always the lateral pull on a big fish which can get the fisherman into the most trouble. This is especially true in the early stages of the battle when the fish is still strong and can effectively respond to it. So, in the early stages, the fisherman should do all he can to keep it to a minimum. Only when the fish is weakening and the end-game is approaching can he afford to neglect doing that.

The question is 'How can he keep the lateral pull to the minimum?' Well, for one thing he can move up to a suitable high point on the bank, if one is available, because from there the angle of the line at the fish will be nearer to the vertical. Not only will this reduce the lateral component of the pull, it will also reduce the amount of line in the water. In its turn this will reduce the hydrodynamic influence on the line and so reduce the lateral pull's magnitude. For another he can move even further upstream because this will tend to have much the same effect. Best of all he can move to a high point which is suitably upstream, and get the combined benefits of both.

Now let us leave the somewhat artificial environment of our peculiar canal and move to a wide, fast-flowing river, thus introducing factors which we have not hitherto taken into account. In a river, unlike our canal, the current will not be uniform. There may be a deep-water channel where the current is strongest, with areas of slacker water on one or both sides of it. There may be rocks and other hazards to worry about. Moreover, the problems of the fisherman's lack of mobility in the early stages will need to be considered, if he happens to be wading when the fish is hooked.

If he is wading near the bank at the time, and can regain it quickly, well and good, but he may be twenty yards or more away from it. In those circumstances he has to be very careful in what he does to regain it, because he will not yet know how big the fish is, or what its potential may be for getting him into trouble while he is still in the water and relatively immobile.

His best course of action is to assume that the fish is well hooked and to endeavour to bring it with him, on as short a line as he can, while he edges his way, a yard or two at a time, towards his goal. By being easy on it during this tricky period, especially if it was lying well below him when it was hooked, he may be able to induce it to swim up towards him, enabling him to recover some of the line out. If he can do that he will be able to move faster towards the bank. A lot of line out at this stage will carry with it too much danger that the influence of the current on it will produce too heavy a lateral pull, and cause the fish to take off for the opposite side of the river. That is the worst thing that could happen because it would result in a very great deal of the line getting into the water, with all the attendant problems. The next worst thing would be for the fish to come upstream too fast, and get upstream of him before he regains his own bank where he could move upstream fast as well. In that event he may have to stay where he is, or even wade further in, so as to keep as near to the fish as practicable in the hope that he can still keep it on a short line and avoid the line becoming drowned.

With big fish the battle is often won or lost at this stage, when the fisherman is still pinned down in the water.

Assuming that he regains his bank successfully and discovers that he is, in truth, involved with a big fish, his best plan is now to play it for a while on the basis of keeping the lateral pull to the minimum as already described. Apart from that, he can now be as hard on it as he likes. If his efforts to minimise the lateral pull are unsuccessful, as regrettably they sometimes are, and the fish does force its way to the other side of the river, he should not hesitate to get well upstream of it because by doing this he will keep the line as far out of danger of fouling intervening rocks as is practicable. Then it is just a matter of waiting for the fish to come back into mid-river again.

Not until the fish starts to come up in the water will it be advisable for him to apply sidestrain to force it into the slacker water on his side of the stream. With a big fish this may entail quite a long wait. Having got it into slacker water he can walk it up or drop it down to the slackest water conveniently at hand where the end-game can be played out and the fish beached, netted or gaffed.

If he has done all these things correctly he will, in my view, have done everything right – but not in the eyes of the Lore. The Lore seems unable to discriminate between big fish and small ones; between wide, fast-flowing rivers and those which are narrow or sluggish; or between playing fish on the fly and playing them on the bait. It lumps them all in together. Consequently its advice is hardly likely to be sound and may even be disastrous. It is interesting to see what it says our fisherman should have done.

He came out of the water as soon as was *practicable*, but the Lore says he should have done so straight away, no matter what.

He waited until the time was ripe before exerting maximum pressure on the fish, but the Lore says he should have done that from the outset.

Until the fish tired and came up in the water he played it from points which were somewhat upstream of it, but the Lore, which has absolutely no conception of the hydrodynamics involved, says that this would only have helped it to rest. In fact the Lore says that as soon as he had got out of the water the fisherman should have taken up a position abreast of or preferably below, his fish. To make it absolutely certain that he would follow this advice in the most dangerous way possible, it actually draws diagrams showing the fish in the water and the fisherman on the bank at an angle of about 45 degrees downstream of it!!

The fisherman refrained from using sidestrain to try to force the fish towards his bank until the time was ripe for that, but the Lore is mad about sidestrain and insists that it is proper to use it from the start. It describes it as exerted by 'lowering the point of the rod to water level in a downstream direction', and as it has already said that the fisherman's optimum position is at an angle of about 45 degrees downstream from his fish the mind boggles at what this would do in the early stages.

The fisherman aimed at getting his fish out of the stream into slacker water as soon as it was appropriate to try to do this, but the Lore says that he should have left it in the stream because that is where it would have tired itself out quickest (although nothing could be further from the truth).

Moreover, the Lore doesn't like a vertical strain because, it says (and with diagrams too), that fish can easily defeat this. It ignores the fact that in the early stages big fish can just as easily defeat sidestrain (or any other kind of strain for that matter). It also ignores the evident truth that the sooner the fish can be brought up in the water the better, because this will lessen the hydrodynamic forces acting on the line and lessen the danger of it drowning or fouling obstructions. Conversely the sidestrain the Lore recommends, if exerted too early, is calculated to increase the dangers of both.

As usual the Lore is intent on persuading the fisherman to behave as foolishly as possible. Anyone following its advice about playing fish may get away with it if the fish is small. If it is a specimen fish in a wide, fast-flowing river, and he does as the Lore prescribes, I'm afraid his chances of landing it can only be assessed as very poor.

24

A Difficult Dee Fish

As usual, after a rise in the river, I went straight to the Moral. This Woodend pool is one of the most beautiful on the Aberdeenshire Dee. Heavily wooded on both banks and liberally garnished with heather and bell-heather, it is comfortably insulated from many of the disturbances of civilisation. Consequently many forms of wild-life are attracted to it and the scene is often as fascinating as it is beautiful. In one way and another I enjoy fishing there more than anywhere else I know.

For example, one can be in such close proximity to roe deer that one could, if so inclined, put the fly over them. These creatures are normally very shy but when they come to the Moral they seem to discard their shyness and a fisher can continue to cast without disturbing them to any marked extent. This never seems to happen anywhere else.

The pool is also a favourite place for birds of prey, and it is not unusual to have buzzards circling overhead, or to be able to watch the occasional kestrel at work. One year, sparrow-hawks were nesting in the trees opposite and the cries of their young greatly disturbed the pool's normal peace. The activities of the parent birds compensated for that, however, and provided enthralling viewing for the solitary fisherman, diverting much of his attention from the task in hand.

Mink are less attractive but equally interesting companions, and will continue to hunt and fish in total disregard of the flexing rod and hissing line. One of the more fascinating sights can be that of a red squirrel dithering over whether or not to cross the river, and then taking the plunge (literally like an Olympic swimmer at the start of a race) when it finally makes up its mind to go.

As for the fish, it is a favourite place for them too. Moreover it has a particular attraction for big fish (big by Dee standards, that is, where the average weight is 9–10 pounds). I have lost more than my fair share of them there; not because it is an especially difficult pool in which to play them but because the water towards the opposite bank is deep and full of submerged rocks, and big fish have an inherent tendency (and ability) to fight their way over to it. When they do, and enter this hazardous area, disaster usually follows.

On the occasion being described, I was well down towards the tail of the pool without having had a touch when suddenly the line tightened and a fish was on. The pool is quite broad at that point, with heavy current towards the opposite bank and a lot of very shallow water on the Woodend side. I was wading up to my waist and so had to edge out, taking the fish with me, otherwise there would have been a risk of the line becoming drowned.

Everything went well at first and the fish came along quite docilely, but with big fish things sometimes do not work out according to plan and at the first sign of the water getting shallow it took off for the far bank, crossing the stream and lashing about in the slacker water among the rocks there, forcing me to wade back in again. In doing this I had to hold the rod high above my head in order to keep as much line out of the water as possible, which made winding in difficult. I was also being hampered by the wading staff, which threatened to trip me up at every step.

By this time I was convinced that the fish was a sizeable one and, as I simply could *not* persuade it to come back to me, began to think that my chances of landing it were slight. However, I edged my way well upstream in order to keep the line as high in the water as possible, and hoped for the best. Nevertheless I kept imagining that the line was foul of rocks, because the fish seemed so immovable, but in the end it always moved and my anxiety eased.

Eventually the fish elected to come back of its own accord, and I was able to get close enough to my own bank to discard the hampering wading staff. All this had taken quite a long time, and now that the immediate dangers had been surmounted I began to worry about the hook pulling out. It will be just another 'lost monster' story for me to recount to my friends, I thought. I tried to decide what it would be best to do next.

It obviously wasn't on to play the fish out where it was, so close to the heavy current where the streamy conditions would have been quite comfortable for it. Nor did it appear possible to walk it up to the head of the pool, where there was an area of slack water, because this was too far away, the fish too big and the current too heavy. So I decided on a compromise – to walk it up part of the way to a point where the beach went in more steeply, although there would be too much current there for my liking. This I eventually managed to do, but not without difficulty, with the fish repeatedly veering out into the heavy stream and the strain on the tackle becoming excessive.

Up to this stage I hadn't been able to get a view of it, or even to assure myself that it was not, after all, a much smaller fish hooked in the back, but now I could see that it was big all right, possibly a 30-pounder, and hooked in the mouth.

Well, I thought, all I have to do now is to let it play itself out more or less where it is, and Bob's your uncle! But not a bit of it! All it did was to lie about ten yards out from the shore, like a battleship at anchor, and do nothing at all.

In the hope of galvanising it into some sort of activity I maintained a heavy strain on it, but it merely used this to keep itself in position, as if it were a paravane. If I eased the strain, or varied the direction of the pull, it just undulated away into the deep water, and then did nothing there. This amounted to a dead loss, because it gave me all the trouble of getting it back again without anything significant having been achieved. So I was forced back on the tactic of holding it in the slacker water on my side of the stream by means of a heavy sideways strain, shouting 'Patience! Patience!' to myself at appropriate intervals.

After a while I thought 'This just cannot go on!', and got my gaff out intending to sneak up on it, but this proved to be quite impossible. If I kept the strain on, there was great danger of breaking the rod. If I didn't, the fish just moved away. So, shouting 'Patience! Patience!' as before, I resorted to the previous tactic of waiting for it to give up.

Time passed, and the situation remained unchanged. At one point I thought that the fish must be aground, with visions of it being about six feet deep. Finally it did touch down, on its side but with its head pointing away from the beach. There was no prospect of hauling it round so that its head was inshore and, as I did not wish to use the gaff, the only alternative seemed to be to try to pull it out backwards by the tail. I hoped that the fish might now be so played out as to make this possible, and should have known better. Big fish are in a class by themselves, and it is never wise to take anything for granted.

Anyway, I gave it a go and got a firm grip on its tail. It immediately became upright in the most miraculous manner and shot off into mid-river, nearly taking me with it. I was soaked from head to foot and spattered with gravel, sand and other muck. So was the reel, which now would hardly turn. I thought the parting had come at last.

Plunging the reel into the water, thinking that this might clean and so clear it, I raised the rod again without much hope only to find that, in spite of everything, all was more or less well. The reel would just turn, and with much grinding and rasping I managed to get back on terms.

The fish had now taken a second lease on life, probably aware for the first time that in spite of its great strength things were not going too well for it. It repeatedly thwarted my efforts to walk it on to the beach, and I became more and more desperate.

Everything has to come to an end some time, however, and at long last the unrelenting strain began to tell. Finally the fish again flopped on its side, its head now inshore, and it was beached. As I walked towards it, grinding in, I was by no means sure that this really was the end, but it was. When I got it by the tail again it no longer responded, and I was able to push it up the shingle to receive the last rites.

I still thought it might be a 30-pounder but, alas, it weighed but a shade under 27 pounds.

It wasn't at all well hooked and I picked the fly out of its mouth as easily as a cherry from a cake. A more active fish would probably have dislodged it long before, and the story would have had its usual unhappy ending.

I then noticed something which, being philosophically and psychologically minded, I found distinctly intriguing. The beautiful Moral had suddenly become even more beautiful than ever! It was hard to credit that such a minor event as the capture of a good fish could bring about such a miracle, but in some subtle and unaccountable way it certainly had.

25

The Strange Behaviour of Tackle Makers and Others

I wonder if any other fisherman has noticed, as I have, that as soon as one finds some item of tackle or gear which is really good, and which one cannot be without, the manufacturer immediately ceases to make it. Conversely, if there is an article which seems to be really unsuitable and should never have been produced in the first place, he will persist with it for years and years, and many is the poor tyro who, not knowing better, will be saddled with it.

I have a list as long as my arm of items falling into one category or the other and, as I have been a good customer of our tackle makers for over fifty years, feel I am entitled to poke a little Charley at them over one or two.

Once upon a time the best salmon fly-reels in the world were made in Britain. They were beautifully designed, ticked like expensive watches and were virtually indestructible. I still have some examples which have given me splended service all my life. How *could* anyone have decided to stop making them in favour of modern fly-reels, many of which (compared with the old ones) are flimsy, raucous and ill-natured? Oh, I admit that the old reels were heavy, but why not make them lighter while still maintaining the integrity of their excellent design? Everyone else appreciated their merit, why didn't the manufacturers? The demand for them must still have existed because, to my knowledge, at least one firm in a far-flung corner of the world immediately started to make replicas. And surely it cannot have been the cost? After all, many people now appear to be prepared to pay hundreds of pounds for a rod, so why should they not put their hands deep in their pockets for a good reel? Especially as a good reel is likely to remain a companion for life, whereas a good rod does not normally last quite that long.

A lesser item which suddenly became unobtainable several years

147

ago was the wading coat. It was simple, well cut and completely effective. It did not boast zips or elaborate pockets and so was relatively inexpensive. In fact it did not need to have pockets at all, because it was worn over the top of one's normal fishing coat when the weather required it. For more years than I can remember I was never without one, as it made me completely weatherproof. In snow or rain it kept me dry because neither could get down inside my breast-waders, or down my neck or up my sleeves. It was absolutely indispensable, and yet when mine wore out and I went along to buy a new one I was told 'The line has been discontinued.'

As luck would have it, I was told that the remaining stock (three) would be in the forthcoming sale, so I bought the lot for a few shillings. One I gave away to someone who deserved it, and who has had great benefit from it ever since; the other two I kept for myself. Both are now unwearable, being in tatters and totally worn out. Oh, how I have missed them, these past three or four years Without them, bad weather has been so hard to bear.

Another version did appear on the market after a time, but it was made of a material which was not impervious to the wet and so was not effective enough. Now, at last, an enterprising manufacturer has reintroduced an example which may be as good as the original, because it is at least waterproof. To my mind it is unnecessarily elaborate, having zips and pockets all adding to its cost, but at least it *should* do the job all right provided that it fits as well as the old one did. So I can say 'Nice one, Cyril!' to that particular manufacturer and, my goodness, that makes a pleasant change.

Another item of gear which has been with me all my life – well, for the past forty years anyway – is my wading staff. I do not know what I would do if I broke or lost it, because it is as indispensable to me as one of my legs. Everything about it is right – its feel, its balance, its length and its weight. Whenever I use any other I become uncertain and uncomfortable. Nevertheless, mine was originally in the second of the two categories mentioned at the beginning of this chapter.

In thinking about how it was when I bought it, all those years ago, I am forced to conclude that fishing-tackle makers used to search around to find wading-staff designers who were totally mad. It is possible that they still do, for all I know, because if there is anything which clinks, clanks, clatters, hums, booms, glints, shines, flashes or is otherwise unsuitable, you may be sure that someone in the lunatic fringe will immediately seize upon it and turn it into a wading staff. Has everyone forgotten Isaak Walton's precept that fishermen should always 'Study to be quiet'?

Take mine, for example, which was on the market for about half a century. It was beautifully made, and great trouble had obviously been taken to make it as unsuitable for its purpose as possible. Not only was it shod with bare iron, but with a very complicated piece of bare iron, like the boat-hook in use in Nelson's day. This had a very long, sharp spike, guaranteed to slide off any rock encountered with as much noise as possible and, if it did not slide off anything, a hook part calculated to hit rock, gravel or shingle with a really good bang. Instead of being called a bang-hook, as it properly should have been, this was known in the trade as a bank-hook, and was designed to help very old gentlemen climb up steep banks. So I imagine that the particular maniac who designed this particular staff must have been in his dotage.

When, after using it for a while and realising its enormous potential for scaring fish, I returned it to the manufacturer for modification, it became perfectly clear that he, too, was well aware of this shortcoming, because he rectified it in very short order. He whipped off the iron contraption, replacing it with rubber-shod lead. This in fact anticipated another of my objections to the staff (of which he must equally well have been aware), namely that the beastly thing had a tendency to be washed from side to side in any appreciable current, clinking and clanking against the stones like a ghost in chains. The weight of the lead now prevented that.

I was so impressed by his efficiency that I completely overlooked his effrontery in marketing such an unsuitable article in the first place.

Again, great care had clearly been taken by the designer in selecting the material of which the shaft was made. This was not only so pale in colour as to make it as noticeable as it could possibly be, but was also extremely and permanently shiny. Not content with that, he must have gone to great lengths to find something with these characteristics which was also hollow. Thus, even when the business end had been modified and become rubber-shod, the staff would still reverberate loudly when it struck anything. Not any old reverberation, either, but a low-frequency one which would carry well through water! I can imagine him being beside himself with satisfaction at having achieved *that*, and thinking 'No one will dare to complain about it for fear of being thought pernickety!'

Well, I did complain about it after a while, and back the staff went for further modification. Again the manufacturer knew exactly what was needed and again it was returned to me, appropriately modified, in double quick time. He had parcelled the staff with thick cord for about half its length, and had stained this dark brown, thereby rendering it comparatively inconspicuous and also killing most effectively those damnable reverberations.

That is how my wading staff became the perfect article it now is. The manufacturer, however, continued to market the original model, with all its shortcomings, for decades!

What is it, do you suppose, which compels our worthy manufacturers to do things which are so incomprehensible to the rest of us? It can't be the bomb, or the welfare state, because the history of their strange behaviour pre-dates both. Could it be the weather?

—— 26 ——

Grilse and Kelts

At first sight, grilse and kelts are unlikely bedfellows, but they do have one particular thing in common, and that is the problem of identifying them quickly and accurately at the waterside.

In the case of grilse, difficulty in doing this has come about because those beautiful little summer fish with small heads, slender wrists and forked tails, to which the name was given in the first instance, were originally thought to be of a different species from salmon. When this became of interest to scientists they proved it to be otherwise. Those gentlemen, by scale examination, were able to define exactly what these little fish were, namely salmon which had returned to fresh water after spending one winter only in the sea. And, whether it was the intention or not, this came to be regarded as the standard definition for grilse, landing us in all sorts of trouble, because it has subsequently been found that much larger fish, indistinguishable at a glance from 2 + fish for example, are also, by definition, grilse. Moreover, if one applies the definition strictly, fish which have spawned and survived to make a second return from the sea, but without having spent a second winter in it, are also grilse. But when *that* is postulated there is an immediate outcry from scientists to the effect that the definition is being applied incorrectly, that it is meant to apply to maiden fish only. I accept that, but it does not alter the fact that, to many fishermen, the definition remains inadequate and needs to be amended, something which they have wanted for years. But there has been no move to amend it, in spite of all the confusion it has created.

This is surprising for several reasons. To take just one, the net returns differentiate between grilse and salmon, but as the definition stands they cannot be accurate. I once asked an expert how the netsmen made this differentiation, because it was obviously impracticable to do it by scale reading, and he gave me to understand that it was merely by weight, once the grilse run had started. If that is so, it is very probable that a number of small summer salmon find themselves included in the figures for grilse, and a number of grilse find themselves included in the salmon figures, making the statistics misleading. Then a netsman tried to persuade me that 'one develops an eye for grilse', but this failed to convince me as likely to be accurate, because I had had a retired netsman as ghillie for several seasons and he was no more reliable than I was when it came to the visual identification of fish which could have been one thing or the other.

To take another reason, the fish market also differentiates between grilse and salmon, treating the former as inferior, certainly as regards price, although they are much better to eat. I believe the market does make the differentiation by eye, and that it is only the small, slender-wristed, fork-tailed fish which are classified as grilse. Consequently it seems likely that some grilse are sold in the market as salmon, making confusion worse confounded, and possibly contravening the Trades Description Act.

Finally, to throw the whole business into complete disarray, it is now being suggested by at least one scientist that some large fish which have apparent 1 + scale readings are, in fact, 2 + fish whose scales (for some unspecified reason) have not registered one of their feeding winters. If that is so, it is not merely the identification of grilse which becomes in doubt, but the whole process of identifying the various classes of salmon, and the validity of scale reading itself.

What does all this matter to a rod-fisherman? Well, some of us, at all events, like to think that our records are reliable, and that when we record our catch we do so with accuracy. I have in mind one particular incident which illustrates what I mean.

On my return to base one day I met a friend who told me that his wife had caught two grilse that afternoon, of 6 and 7 pounds respectively, which were as beautiful to look at as any fish he had ever seen. The head ghillie was at hand and the three of us went to inspect these fish and admire them. They certainly were magnificent, as fresh as daisies and with marvellous shapes. I turned to my friend and said 'Yes, they are perfectly beautiful, but are you sure they are grilse? In my records they would be entered as salmon.' The head ghillie agreed. 'Yes, definitely small summer salmon,' he said. 'You've only got to look at their tails.' My friend thereupon decided to send scales from each to be examined, and told me later that the answer was that they were both grilse.

As matters stand, the only 1 + fish which the angler can easily identify are the small, slender-wristed, fork-tailed ones, which were originally given the name grilse. Others return from the sea in more advanced stages of maturity, presumably depending on the feeding conditions they have encountered there, and these he cannot readily identify. Moreover he can only identify the former, by eye, when they are fresh-run, because the maturing process appears to continue in fresh water, and they lose their 'grilsey' characteristics after a few weeks in the river. This may be the explanation for the apparent phenomenon of grilse running into a river and 'disappearing', which has so often been an occasion for comment.

To sum up, I (in common with many ordinary anglers) am unconcerned as to whether the fish I catch are 1 +, 2 +, 3 + or 4 + fish, and have no particular desire to differentiate between them in my records. What I *do* want is to be able to record those marvellous little fish which were originally classified as grilse, and which can be seen to be grilse at a casual glance, without invalidating my records as a whole. I resent the name 'grilse' being given to all 1 + fish, as it has been, just because this is of some interest to statisticians, and hope very much that somehow, some day, the present definition will come to be rationalised in a way which satisfies everybody.

With kelts the problem is the same but different, if you will forgive the paradox. It is not the definition of a kelt which clouds the issue in any way, but the straightforward problem of identifying kelts by eye, especially if one is lacking in experience. I do not mean experience in general but particular experience in identifying kelts. That is why a ghillie, who spends the whole of every spring on a water, is better at it than the average rod who spends only a week or two, however experienced he may be in other ways.

Why then, I wonder, is the average salmon fisher so infuriated by the implication that he cannot reliably tell the difference between a fish and a kelt? You might as well impugn his honour! He will never admit that he is capable of a misjudgement, and when he has actually made one will take a lot of convincing that he has actually done so. There is nothing to be ashamed of in making a genuine mistake, but just try telling him that!

Sometimes the error arises because he is taken off guard, for example by the isolated and unexpected kelt encountered in late April, but more often than not it is because his experience is insufficiently comprehensive, which he will be unwilling to admit.

I used to be thoroughly convinced that I could tell kelts from fish without the slightest difficulty. I had done so often enough, and there seemed to be no problem. Then, and it is many years ago now, I had a nasty shock to my pride. It was February, and I had hooked what seemed to be a perfectly normal fish, which gave me a lot of trouble because it was big and there was deep, fast water up against the bank from which I was fishing. I never got a proper view of this fish at all, while playing it, and when at last I got it close under the bank and had an opportunity to gaff it, I did so. As a rule I never use the gaff, especially in the spring, unless it is absolutely necessary, but in this instance there seemed to be no alternative. There was nothing in my mind to suggest that I might be involved with a kelt, or I would have acted differently.

As soon as I had got it on the bank, however, I was filled with horror, as it had every indication of being a kelt, even to traces of fungus here and there on its flanks. If I had not gaffed it I would have put it back just to be on the safe side. As it was, I didn't know what to do. I dared not face the rest of the party with it, in case it was a kelt, even though there were mitigating circumstances. I knew that, if it was, I would be chaffed unmercifully and made to feel that I was a murderer. Moreover I suddenly remembered that I had hooked it in a pool which was notorious for harbouring kelts and cursed myself for having failed to remember that before. So I decided to take it away and bury it, and to expunge the whole incident from my mind as something best forgotten. With the benefit of hindsight, I doubt very much whether it was, in fact, a kelt.

Some years later this incident was forcibly recalled because I had another, similar, shock to my pride. Again it was a fish which gave me a lot of trouble and again I was in considerable doubt as to its identity when finally I got it ashore. But this time I had had more experience of spring fishing, and knocked it on the head with a fair amount of confidence because I felt that no kelt could possibly have put up such a fight. But once I had done so misgivings started to set in. It had a horribly keltish look. So I decided to apply the criteria which I believed would provide a reliable indication:

Its head was large and out of proportion to its body. Kelt!
Its body lacked plumpness. Kelt!
Its shape was bad. Kelt!
Its gills were pale and maggoty. Kelt!
Its fins and tail were ragged. Kelt!
Its vent seemed to protrude easily. Kelt!
It was dull and slightly dirty-looking and there was no 'bloom'. Kelt!

I was filled with misery, which stayed with me for the whole of the rest of the day. It seemed that I had done it again.

However, I screwed up my courage and decided on a different course of action from the one I had taken before. I certainly was not going to put the creature in the sink at the end of the day, with all that it might let me in for, but this time I was going to try and learn something before I buried it.

So I determined that, when the time came to pack up, I would call at the ghillie's cottage and show it to him. And if he was out, as I feared he might be, I would find someone else whose judgement I respected, and ask him. In the event the ghillie was in, pronounced it to be an undeniable fish, and sent it off to market with the others.

I was telling the story that evening to a fellow angler who was on his way home after a fortnight on the Spey. He told me that, amazingly enough, he had just had an almost identical experience. He had landed a fish which, although strong when in the water, had every indication of being a kelt when he was able to examine it on the bank. He had therefore decided to return it, and was just about to do so when the ghillie came along and congratulated him on his fish.

Now we happened, that evening, to be having a dram with a retired ghillie, and he had listened to our stories with amusement. His comment on them was that, in his belief, rods, fishing on their own, returned quite as many fish to the water, in the mistaken belief that they were kelts, as kelts were knocked on the head in the mistaken belief that they were fish.

When I returned home after this second shock, I was determined to comb my library for everything that had ever been written about identifying kelts so as to repair the obvious gaps in my experience. When I had finished this rather limited piece of research I was left with the distinct impression that the writers knew no more about the subject than I did. Some of them obviously knew considerably less. Some of them trotted out the same old list of things to look for, which I knew from experience was not only useless but positively misleading, and others seemed intentionally vague. In one book I found that the whole section on kelts had been lifted, word for word, out of another book published some seventy years earlier!

The only really valid observation contained in any of the books I read was that experience was the only reliable guide. With it, the authors said, one could make the judgement on 'general impression' with a fair amount of confidence. One writer suggested, in this connection, that a kelt 'never looked you straight in the eye', and I liked that because it is true that kelts do have a sort of hangdog look, as though thoroughly ashamed of themselves. Although accurate enough, these observations were not likely to be of much help to the tyro or the inexperienced, and they were not of any immediate help to me either. It seemed that the man who claims never to have mistaken a kelt for a fish, or vice versa, may be dismissed as a liar. In other words, one just has to learn the difference between the two the hard way.

This is how it has been for me, and I now have the confidence which comes with experience. I never bother with the standard and oft-repeated criteria, as I believe these to be just a waste of time. This is probably just as well because I have had kelts whose gills were blood-red and maggot-free and whose fins and tails were dark and immaculate. I rely entirely on general impression, starting with the moment of hooking. Everything else being equal, a kelt will never fight very well, or for very long, whatever the circumstances, unless of course one is fishing with tackle which is unsuitable for the early spring. If not properly equipped, one can easily be misled, so there is a moral there. Also there will be far less difficulty in keeping a kelt near the surface, and its fight will tend to be thoroughly splashy from the outset. With appropriately strong tackle one will seldom be fooled, even by a big kelt in heavy water, if one plays it properly. On occasion, I admit, I have found that what had given me the impression of being a kelt turned out to be a small, tired, fresh fish, but this was just a pleasant surprise and no harm was done.

Occasionally I am still in doubt up to the moment of landing the creature but once it is on the bank 'general impression' usually dispels that doubt immediately. Only very seldom do I now have recourse to my final test, which is one of weight. A kelt will always feel light, in the hand, for its size. If it does not, you may be sure it is a fish. In that connection, do not trouble yourself over the term 'well-mended', as often applied to kelts, because it is an unfortunate and misleading one. Kelts do not mend in fresh water, in the sense that they regain condition to any noticeable extent. They merely revert to a silvery colour and, possibly, the sides of the void left by their extruded ova or milt come together sufficiently to disguise its presence. Weight is therefore a reliable guide if you are sufficiently experienced to use it. As you must be a good judge of it, if it is to be of help, never pass up an opportunity of estimating a fish's weight in normal circumstances and checking your accuracy. Once you can do it to within half a pound or so you'll have no further trouble with kelts.

To sum up again, there is really no substitute for experience when it comes to differentiating between kelts and fish, and no rule of thumb can help the tyro or those who have never done much fishing in the early spring. If, however, someone was to put a pistol to my head and say 'Give them *some* advice – or else!' I would, with reluctance and great diffidence, offer the following.

If your catch is bright, and you are in doubt about it, the chances are that it is a kelt, which you must, by law, return unharmed to the water. A bright *fish*, with its small head, better shape and (if really fresh) violet bloom, would have been unmistakable.

If it is red, and you are in doubt about it, you can knock it on the head with a fair amount of confidence because the chances are that it is a fish all right or, alternatively, a baggot. A red kelt is such a miserable-looking creature that it would normally leave you in no doubt as to its identity. Moreover, you will be able to push your fingers into its 'soft underbelly' – the void left by its extruded milt or ova – and that will be a dead give-away.

If it is neither bright nor red and not, unmistakably, a fish or a kelt, apply the weight test to the best of your ability and make your ultimate judgement on that.

I wish you luck!

27

Improving a Fishery

Some years ago I was asked by a firm of architects to advise on the facilities required for a salmon fishery. Since then the theme of improving fisheries has occupied my thoughts from time to time. How marvellous it would be, I think to myself, to be given *carte blanche* on some water, and a substantial backing in cash to go with it! What loving care I would lavish on the job! When I had finished it the whole world would beat a path to the water to see how everything should be. And having got everything right my next objective would be to ensure that it all remained that way, and that the fishery was properly maintained.

An example of a well appointed and well kept fishery is Broadlands, and it is always a pleasure to fish there for that very reason. In some ways its maintenance is more difficult than that of, say, a Highland river, but in others it is easier because, being pastoral, access is easier. The increased difficulty arises because control of weed-beds is involved, together with everything that goes with weed cutting, for example foot-bridges, nets and their associated gear. There is also a lot of timberwork to be maintained at Broadlands, including numbers of groynes and catwalks. A feature of the latter, often neglected elsewhere, is the care taken to give them a non-slip surface by the use of chicken netting, which needs to be replaced as soon as it starts to break up otherwise it could become a hazard. There are bridges for vehicles as well as foot-bridges to be looked after, and one of them was recently completely rebuilt. The huts are always in apple-pie order, and some of them have a feature which is particularly comforting – an outside Elsan lavatory. As for the banks, I do not know the precise figure but I would guess that there is a total of about ten miles of them to be kept in order. This is not a simple job, because cattle have access to them along most of their length, but it is always well done.

All in all, it is a fishery where maintenance is taken seriously and managed properly. It is a credit to Bernard Aldrich, the head river keeper, and to the Broadlands Estate as a whole.

Not many fisheries compare well with Broadlands in this respect. The will to do so seems to be lacking. I suppose it must be the great cost of everything these days, because anything which requires much expenditure seems continually to be deferred. This is a great mistake. The work may be put off but it will have to be done in the end and will then be much more costly. When banks begin to break up they should be repaired at once and not left until it becomes a major engineering effort to restore them. It is the same with trees. Regular pruning is no great task but leave them to overgrow the river and it becomes necessary to call in a team of lumberjacks to put things right. Comparatively minor growth on banks, if not regularly and adequately controlled, has a nasty habit of transforming itself into a great robust jungle, almost while one's back is turned, which can only be removed with great difficulty. As for roads, huts, stiles, gates, groynes, rod-boxes, catwalks, bridges, and so on, if they are not given, consistently, the comparatively small amount of maintenance that they require, they will have to be remade, rebuilt or otherwise replaced sooner or later at many times the cost. The old saw that the ship can be spoiled for a ha'porth of tar may be trite, but nowhere is it more true than in its application to a fishery.

So I think the first thing I would do, with this fantasy water of mine, would be to put its maintenance on to a sound, planned basis. I would rely on the ghillie only for those minor jobs which were well within his capabilities and encourage him to keep a list of all the other things that needed to be done. I would not just leave it at that, but would walk the water with him from time to time to check his list and, perhaps, add items of my own. Then, at the end of the season, or at any other convenient time, I would sit down with him and draw up the programme of work, together with the labour it would need, to be carried out during the next twelve months. A costly process? Not at all. Planned maintenance has been proved, over and over again, to be a genuine money-saver. As it has been found to make good sense everywhere else, why not with a fishery? A good water is such a tremendous asset these days that it deserves to be managed and maintained with care and intelligence.

Good access is important to good maintenance and I would next turn my attention to that. Ghillies are only human, and if a job needs

159

to be done but the ghillie knows that all the materials, tools and equipment needed to do it will have to be carried on his back for several hundred yards over difficult terrain, he will tend to put off the evil day for as long as possible. It is most noticeable that fisheries with good access are generally in much better shape than those without it, and those with the priceless advantage of having a virtually all-weather track for vehicles running along their entire length are the best kept of all. Money spent on providing good access is therefore money well spent, and will be recouped over the years from the dividends to be derived from good maintenance.

That is not the only advantage it confers, either. The fishers will bless it too. Nothing destroys breast-waders so quickly and completely as having to walk long distances in them, along overgrown paths perhaps, and in these days, when it is possible to pay over £100 for a pair of good waders, that is quite a significant consideration. It also goes without saying that anything which saves fishers the effort that has to be expended in carrying gear, and fish, over long distances is calculated to increase their chances of success and consequently their enjoyment. Good access is very important to them.

Huts are worth more than just casual consideration because there are many factors which affect the ideal. Geographically, it is desirable to have one on every beat, so placed and designed that a good view of the river is enjoyed as well as shelter from the weather. If the river is one affected by grue, fishers in the early part of the year may be forced to spend long periods in huts, while waiting for the grue to go off, so they then require some form of heating. It is unnecessary for this to be elaborate, involving fireplaces, stoves and chimneys. Calor gas heaters are quite adequate for outlying huts, and these have been installed with notable success on some fisheries with which I am acquainted.

The design of main huts – those which are going to be used as a base and where gear, food and drink are liable to be left overnight – needs much more care, nowadays, than it used to get. In general, existing huts are altogether too easily broken into and positively invite this form of undesirable activity in consequence. Very little is needed in the way of burglary prevention, however, to turn this into a major operation. Doors should have strong locks of the mortice type and be so constructed that they cannot be jemmied open or the lock cut out. As an aid to this, the striker-plate should be of thick metal, running the whole length of the door-jamb, and be secured in place with plenty of good-sized screws. The door itself should be backed with metal and the lock secured to this, so that it could only be cut out with a blow torch. The hinge side should not be forgotten and should embody metal claws which, when the door is shut, engage in a long metal plate on the door-jamb, similar to the striker plate on the lock side. Windows are comparatively easy to make burglar-proof. In this connection shutters are just useless as they can easily be broken open and are a nuisance in other ways. Instead, lockable metal-framed windows should be used, glazed with small panes of Bandit glass, which is virtually unbreakable. In existing windows, Georgian-wired glass could be used instead and still constitute, at least, a powerful deterrent.

In my exercise with the architects, we were more concerned with the facilities to be provided in a small fishing lodge than with anything else, and my advice was that these should comprise four separate spaces: a fish-house, a rod-room, a drying-room and a workshop.

To take the fish-house first, care should be taken to position it so that the direct rays of the sun do not impinge on any part during the heat of the day. It should have good natural ventilation, but natural light is unnecessary. The walls should be tiled up to head height and it should have a tiled, stone or bitumen floor, preferably the latter because of its relatively non-slip character. The lighting should be fluorescent, switched from the outside, with a red tell-tale to warn when the lighting had been left on. There should be a strong-point in the ceiling from which suitable apparatus for weighing fish could be suspended. A large, shallow, white, ceramic sink should be provided, with cold water laid on to it, in which fish could be washed or temporarily stored. This should have a drained zinc surface on one side of it where fish could be displayed, cleaned or cut up. There should be a wall-mounted desk-top for the rough record-book, with a drawer under it for labels, string, etc., and a lockable wall-mounted cupboard for the storage of fish-mats, polythene bags and the like. Facilities for the disposal of offal should exist, preferably in the form of a thick paper bag suspended from a wall-mounted frame positioned at a suitable height. Racks for knives and saws required for cutting up fish should be wall-mounted, and handy. Finally the fish-house should be equipped with a sizeable deep freezer for long-term storage.

I make no apology for giving this specification, although I am sure it will contain nothing new to the readers of this book. Not a single fish-house with which I am familiar possesses all the desirable features, so it is no bad thing to have them comprehensively listed somewhere.

It is much the same thing with rod-rooms and workshops. A rod-room must be dry but should not be heated. In contrast with the fish-house, which can be situated separate from, but adjacent to, the house, the rod-room needs to be part of the house. It should have direct access from the outside and be so designed that long rods can be carried into it, at the trail, and placed in the racks without complicated manoeuvres which may damage them. It should have appropriate racks for hanging up waders, rods in bags, clothing, gaffs, wading staffs and the like. To be truly convenient it should also have a built-in seat to assist one in pulling on or pulling off waders, and some form of work-top on which items of gear or equipment can be temporarily placed. Finally, it should have very good artificial and natural lighting.

The workshop, on the other hand, must be heated, and there should be access to it from both the house and the rod-room. It should be regarded as a place where all the other gear, not already mentioned, will be stowed and should therefore be amply provided with cupboards, racks and shelves. It must contain a good-length work-bench with a vice, and its other features will depend on what activities are likely to be carried out in it. If the occupier will be tying his own flies, for example, there must be a fly-tying bay where there is first-class natural and artificial light with a lower bench at which he can sit. If he intends to make his own baits he will need machine tools, such as a lathe and a power-driven carborundum wheel. Appropriate mountings and power supplies for these must be planned, with plenty of electrical outlets elsewhere as well, especially along the bench. If he is going to go in for rod building or repairing, the facilities for that will need to be planned. Last, but not necessarily least, it should be remembered that a workshop of this kind needs to be regarded as one of the reception rooms of the house, where fishers will inevitably gather to examine gear and talk, so comfortable seating will not come amiss. The more the thought put into designing rod-rooms and workshops the better the result will be.

Little needs to be said about the drying-room, as its function is self-evident. It should have sufficient hanging space to accommodate everyone's wet clothing as and when required, and have suitable controllable heating so that everything can be dried within a reasonable time, say eight hours. Access to it is best provided from the rod-room, so that sopping wet articles do not have to be taken through the workshop or house.

As for the rest of the perfect fishery, there are a number of features, often lacking elsewhere, on which I would insist. Some of them are luxuries, and some essential.

A reliable and appropriately situated wind-vane is one, because it can be very helpful in planning one's strategy when winds are high.

Cattle-grids on access roads may be expensive to install initially, but have become much more competitive now that many people are fitting the newfangled metal anti-cattle gates which are so complicated and costly. Grids virtually last for ever, and save so much in gate maintenance. They are also very much more reliable than gates, as they cannot be left open by some absent-minded fisher, as sometimes happens. Indeed the very complications of the new gates can be disadvantageous, because there are people who do not understand their intricacies, and leave them incorrectly fastened and therefore vulnerable. As for the fishers, there is no doubt which of the two they would prefer, and this is worth considering, at least. Getting in and out of a vehicle in breast-waders in order to open and shut gates can be very tiresome at the end of a hard day or, indeed, at any time.

One of the most important items, however, is the marker or gauge. To have one single master gauge, which it is only possible to consult at the beginning and end of the day, is not enough in my opinion. Knowing the precise height of water at a given pool when deciding whether the pool is likely to be fishing at its best or not is so important that having to rely on a gauge some distance, maybe miles, away from it is unsatisfactory. Rivers change to some extent all the time, and the relationship between the actual height at a pool and that registered at a master gauge at some distant point can change appreciably without this being realised. I take a reading from two widely separated gauges almost every day for months on end, and this has led me to discover that the difference between the two is constantly changing. For a start, it seems to vary with given heights of river, but the average difference seems also to change from season to season. When I first started taking my readings I felt confident that the average difference between the two gauges was 8 inches, then I found that it had become 9 inches and now it is 12 inches or more. It is possible, for all I know, that these two gauges originally read the same.

Anyway, I don't think it is adequate to have to rely on just one gauge when fishing pools which may be several river-miles away. Therefore, in my ideal fishery, I would install a gauge for every pool, or groups of closely associated pools, constructed in such a way that it could easily be read from both sides of the river and did not require to be continually repainted and so constitute a maintenance burden. Where the deep water was against the opposite bank the consent of its owner would be needed, but I see no reason why his co-operation should not be forthcoming, as such a gauge would be of value to both sides. Then one would really know what was going on in a given pool and, moreover, one could record more accurately than at present the height of the river when each fish is caught. Without that accuracy one is denied knowledge which can be vital. On some pools on some waters a single inch can make a tremendous difference to potential productivity, even a crucial one.

When it comes to improving a fishery from the point of view of the fish rather than the fisher, difficulties arise and one begins to skate on very thin ice. A very great deal has been written on the subject and not much of it is to be trusted. There have been successes, it is true, but these are overshadowed by the colossal list of expensive failures which one seldom hears about. Very much depends on what one is trying to do and on the type of river in which one is trying to do it.

In the comparatively narrow and lazy chalk-streams of the south, where it is necessary to guard against bank erosion and the accumulation of silt, it may be possible to take the necessary measures without endangering the well-being of the fish. In fact fish may positively benefit from them. Those Broadlands groynes are a good example of this. They not only protect the banks by deflecting the flow towards mid-river, and concentrating it so that it scours well, but in many instances they have created comfortable lies as well. What they are doing is effectively to narrow and so deepen the channel, which is beneficial all round.

It is said of these rivers that they are never subject to spates. Someone said of the Avon, for example, beside which she spent her school-days, that she had never seen it in flood. I cannot say that this never happens today, because I have seen the Test at Broadlands overflowing its banks on occasion, but I dare say it is a rare occurrence. The point is that the effect of groynes on these rivers can be reliably forecast because only seldom are they likely to become submerged. On the other hand, obstructions of this sort which can be submerged in a high water, and regularly are, can have an effect which cannot be forecast and may be disastrous.

Similarly, there have been spectacular successes in improving some sluggish and featureless stretches of the Wye, in which fish would not previously lie, by placing groups of boulders or concrete blocks at intervals on an otherwise level river bed. It is equally true, however, that attempts to create lies for fish in this way have not met with the same success elsewhere. Moreover, if this sort of thing is done on too great a scale there is a distinct risk of the overall effect being an undesirable one, as there is always the possibility that such underwater obstructions, because that is what they are, will cause an eventual change in the location of the deep-water channel and so damage or destroy existing lies in water above and below.

It seems that success in creating lies where none exist is best achieved where the obstructions being placed in the river are likely to subside into the river bed. For this reason, groups of concrete spheres have sometimes been recommended as suitable for a non-rocky bottom, because their shape will encourage scouring around them, and in consequence they will sink until only their top halves, or less, remain protruding above the bottom. Certainly, in my experience, fish often lie behind shallow rounded stones, much preferring them to larger features such as boulders and rocks which protrude more, so there seems to be some sense in this. Clearly the improvement, if any, may not come about for some time after such spheres have been placed in position, and it may be years before it can be determined whether the enterprise has been successful or not.

It is not only in connection with obstructions in the water that pastoral rivers have an advantage. Where there are weed-beds fish are less dependent on the shade provided by trees for their well-being than is the case elsewhere, and their banks can be cleared without running any great risk. The same cannot be said for weed-less rivers, and the trees on their banks which provide shade for fish should never be cut down if this can possibly be avoided. Pruning is all right, provided that it is done with due regard to maintaining more or less intact the total shadow cast, but as far as possible nothing more drastic should ever be undertaken. Indeed, it is often well worth considering planting trees along pools where fish are likely to be too exposed to the sun, as it can only have a beneficial effect in the end. What is more, in these days when everyone seems to get grants for everything, it could be done comparatively cheaply.

In contrast with the slower, pastoral rivers, interfering with those with a rapid fall, and consequently a fast flowing and powerful stream, should be listed among the seven deadly sins. It is as attractive as many of them, and more tempting than most. So great is the temptation, in fact, that I have often wondered if I would be strong-minded enough to resist it, were I ever in charge of such a water, although I am perfectly well aware of the dangers. It would be so easy to look at a pool, say, and think to oneself that if only one did this or that it would clearly fish better or hold more fish. How disastrous the consequences might be if one yielded!

Consider what happens in such rivers when they are in spate. Tons and tons of shingle and gravel are then picked up by the rushing water and carried downstream in semi-suspension, to be deposited again when the speed of the current falls below a certain rate. It is inevitable, therefore, that spates will cause changes, and the fact that these are usually comparatively small, and that the characteristics of a fishery remain reasonably constant, is because a state of precarious equilibrium has been reached in the river over the years. Loose material removed from one spot by the spate, as it builds up, is replaced by that removed from elsewhere and deposited again as the spate dies down. The undesirable consequences of one spate, if any, are often cancelled out by the next. Only occasionally is there some disastrous change.

If this comparatively natural order of things is interfered with at some point or other, there is no saying what the consequences might be. Obstructions, even small ones, have an accelerating and a decelerating effect on running water which may cause the build-up or scouring of loose material to become progressive. Banks of shingle can build up very quickly and alter the course of the deep-water channel or, at worst, cause the whole river to change its course.

When I see someone nibbling away at his water, building croys

166

here and there, or removing some awkward obstruction which has been in existence for thousands, maybe millions, of years I am naturally anxious, especially where these things are done at or near a narrow point in the river. What he is doing may be very well intentioned, but good intentions are not enough. In seeking for some problematical advantage he may be putting good pools, above and below, at risk. It is particularly agonising if what he is doing is to interfere with an existing good pool with the intention of making it better. Often enough he will be destroying or modifying the very feature which caused it to be a good pool in the first place.

Be very wary, therefore, of doing anything, or permitting it to be done, however harmless it might seem, without first taking the very best advice obtainable. The only person really qualified to give it would be a hydraulics expert who understood fish and was also thoroughly familiar with the water. Such a person is likely to be rare, and the possibility of finding him remote. If you did find him, and he was able to give you the very best possible advice, I would be surprised if this wasn't 'Don't!' So perhaps it would be simpler just to anticipate this and act accordingly.

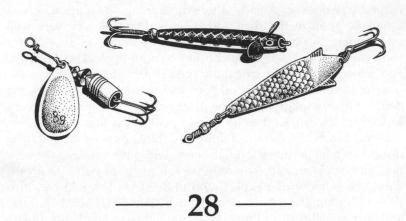

28

Spinning

The Aberdeenshire Dee is, *par excellence*, a river for the fly-fisher. I know of no other salmon river in the world which offers so much incomparable fly water. Yet it was not until I was invited to fish it that I found myself obliged to start fishing the bait. Up to that moment I had spun seriously only for pike, using very clumsy tackle, and had come to the conclusion that it was a method of fishing which I did not particularly enjoy. The idea that I would be expected to employ it when I came to the Dee couldn't have been further from my mind when I accepted my host's kind invitation, and it was only as an afterthought that I took spinning gear with me at all. This took the shape of a little 7-foot greenheart rod, together with one of the earliest Altex reels ever made, and was actually a trout-spinning outfit, given to me a year or two previously, to which Hardy's had added one of the new monofilament nylon lines.

It was therefore with the gravest misgivings that I heard my host say, when he greeted me at Potarch, that the river was in flood and that we would have to spin until it fell to more normal levels.

All went well for a day or two. We fished the fly and the bait (golden sprats) alternately and both were successful. The little trout outfit seemed to work quite well and I was beginning to enjoy using it. Then – disaster! I was playing a fish on the bait when there was a loud crack and the drum of the Altex reel, made of ebonite I think, collapsed.

I suppose the fish was lost, but I cannot now remember. What I do remember, quite indelibly, was my host's remark when I showed him the damage. He said 'When invited to the Dee, Philip, the very least you can do is to equip yourself properly!' This chastening remark I took very much to heart.

When I returned south I therefore set about equipping myself suitably for spinning for salmon. As a start, I got hold of all the books on the subject that I could find and read them from cover to cover. The first thing to be decided was the type of reel I should go for, because on that depended the type of rod I would need. I had had experience of both centre-pin and fixed-spool reels, so it was not a question of which might be the easier to use but, rather, which might be the more suitable. In the end I decided on the multiplier for two reasons. These, to my mind, are just as valid today as they were then.

The first reason was that the fixed-spool reel, although ingenious and certainly the most suitable for casting very light baits, had basic shortcomings. As a piece of engineering designed for playing fish, as opposed to making casts, it seemed to smack too much of Mr Heath Robinson. The design of the multiplier, on the other hand, was perfectly sound for playing fish. As I knew that the baits I would be required to cast were not likely to be ultra-light, the multiplier therefore seemed preferable on engineering grounds.

The second reason was that, almost without exception, fixed-spool reels have a basic design peculiarity, namely that the slipping clutch forms part of the spool assembly instead of being associated, as it should logically be, with the bail. Even today, all fixed-spool salmon reels on the market with which I am familiar have this intrinsic quirk in design, and I have never been able to understand why. Because of it one is able, by operating the handle to 'wind in' while the clutch associated with the spool is slipping, to kink the line most severely. As this is easy enough to do in the heat of the moment, and as a severely kinked line can be incapacitating, I consider this to be the deciding factor against using such a reel when fishing for salmon, although I am aware that many people do get on with it to their satisfaction.

Having decided on the multiplier as the best reel to use – a choice I have never regretted – it now became a question of obtaining the best rod to go with it. In one of the books I read, the author had actually laid down the characteristics of the perfect rod to go with a multiplier and, as what was perfect seemed good enough for me, I decided to have such a rod made. If I remember correctly, the author specified that almost all the action should be in its butt, and that the top joint should bend very little during the act of casting. I trusted him implicity. I therefore took the book to the best rod maker in the country at that time, and ordered a rod 'just like that'. In due course it was delivered, and looked beautiful. On the butt the maker had inscribed 'The P.P.M.G. Special', and this made my bosom swell with pride!

Unfortunately it was to swell with something else when I actually put the rod to use. The makers had done their job perfectly, and the action of the rod was precisely as specified when waggled in the hand. But fishing with it was altogether another matter. As may be supposed, it simply did not have enough action and to get it working it was necessary to introduce a considerable punch into the casting process. I did not like this at all, but thought I might get used to it in time. The crunch came when I hooked a fish. Imagine trying to play it properly on a spinning rod in which most of the action was in the butt and hardly any in the top joint! It was practically impossible. So, when I returned south again, I traded it in for a standard spinning rod with a more conventional action. Poor P.P.M.G. Special!

There is a lesson about rod design in all this, which is that it is a matter best left to those who understand it, as it is not a suitable subject for the dabbling of amateurs or pseudo-professionals. My advice, therefore, to someone having difficulty in finding a rod to suit him from among all those available on the market, and there are enough of these in all conscience, is just to go on trying. It is most unlikely that he will be able to do any better by having yet another one built to some strange specification of his own.

As for the rest of the tackle, experience over the years has gradually led me to hold certain firm convictions about it. In this regard, spinning differs from fly-fishing in one fundamental way, namely the liability to variation in the distance cast. If everything is not geared to obtain consistency, pools will be covered in a way which is just hit-and-miss. Target practice in some suitable open space will soon bring to light all the factors which contribute to it, and is a worthwhile exercise for that reason alone.

The first thing on which it seems desirable to concentrate, in order to achieve consistency, is the swing. Unlike casting the fly, where wind is a problem which obliges one constantly to make adjustments in timing and so on, a standard swing can be developed for casting a bait. In that respect it resembles golf. One can get 'in the groove', so to speak, so that every swing is the exact replica of the one before. In achieving this it is necessary to realise that one must opt to cast well within one's capability and not to strive for maximum distance. With a multiplier this is particularly important because of the centrifugal brake. Of course this could be rendered inactive, and some people do just that, but my own preference is to retain it in operation because it can be so useful at times. But there is no doubt that, with it, to attempt to cast a comparatively light bait too far becomes a highly undesirable thing to do. The more one strives for maximum length the more the brake will come into play and curtail the distance the bait travels. So, apart from introducing inconsistencies in distance, which depend on the vagaries of the centrifugal brake, it is also a waste of effort to try to make very long casts with a light bait. I therefore believe that in casting with a multiplier the aim should be to develop a standard swing with a suitable rod which will bring the brake into play as little as practicable while at the same time propelling the bait to an adequate and consistent distance. If one is continually changing rods, lines or bait weights this will be quite difficult to achieve, so it is best to find those which are suitable and then stick to them.

Another factor affecting distance, and therefore consistency, is the thickness of the line. A thin line will enable a greater distance to be obtained with the standard swing than will a thicker one. Therefore the aim in this case should be to select the thinnest line which is adequate for the conditions likely to be encountered, and get used to it. If this is not done, changes in line thickness will affect the standard swing and one will be at sixes and sevens trying to restore the situation. Of course, in the early spring on a northern river, when there is liable to be ice in the water and ice forming in the rod-rings or even on the line, it is sensible to use a thicker line than, say, in high summer. Care should be taken, though, not to overcorrect for this by using a thicker line than is absolutely necessary to offset the added wear and tear, or distance will be lost unnecessarily and trouble with maintaining the standard swing will again arise.

Finally there is the weight of the bait, which influences distance and so consistency. For some reason, tackle manufacturers are precise about the weight of the spoons they market but do not bother to be equally so where the weight of devons is concerned. It is therefore quite practicable to have weight-matched sets of spoons, even though they have been assembled from different manufacturers, but if devons are obtained from different sources their weights are liable to vary considerably despite their being of the same size. I therefore, as far as I can, use devons of one size only and obtain them from the same source, their shells weighing about half an ounce.

I have grown to be particular about their shape also, disliking those which are tadpole in shape and preferring those where the greatest diameter is at the mid-point in their length, with the fins positioned there too, so that they will swim on an even keel and not in a tail-down posture as does the tadpole. Moreover, I take advantage of the fact that maximum diameter affects the level at which they will fish and have my devons made for me in three categories – slim, normal and pregnant. The difference in weight between one category and another is negligible because the weight mainly reposes in the copper tube, which is standard in each, so consistency is not lost when changing from a bait in one category to a bait in another.

The advantage of having three categories of devon is pretty obvious. If one is fishing a pool where the devon is hanking up too frequently, although little or no lead is being employed, a change to one with a larger diameter will be sufficient to keep one out of trouble without recourse to winding in. It is no use striving to achieve consistency in distance if one then has to wind in from time to time in order to keep off the bottom. In other words, the devon is best fished as one would fish the fly, with winding in normally reserved for recovery only.

This is not so with the spoon, which, I have found, is much more successful if fished high in the water, especially if this is streamy, except when water temperatures are very low. In the summer it can be particularly effective fished very near the surface, and fast. Winding in can therefore be a very necessary feature of fishing the spoon.

Tactics with a spinning bait are now very different from those normally employed in the past. In the old days, when the Silex or Ariel type of centre-pin reel was current, a great deal of lead had to be used, willy-nilly, in order to make good casts, and naturally the bait always fished close to the bottom. When the modern reels appeared, and the amount of lead used became a matter of choice, the idea that the bait should be fished near the bottom persisted, and many people still firmly believe that it is essential for success. It is one of the tenets of our old enemy the Lore, in fact, that one should fish the bait at such a depth as to feel the lead 'bumping the bottom'. This certainly is not so except when the water is very cold, and the preferred tactics with devons in warmer water are now to adjust everything so that the bait comes round with a clear swing in mid-water. In my experience, this is no less successful than the old method and has the advantage of not disturbing fish unduly or, worse, foul-hooking them, which is so time-wasting. Moreover, it is a much more pleasant way to fish because there is less chance of hanking up.

Over the years I have therefore found myself using less and less lead for summer spinning. Nowadays in the summer I normally employ only the tiniest Hillman pea or dispense with lead altogether in favour of a perspex anti-kink vane. A minor modification in technique is required, however, in order to get the unweighted devon to sink as quickly as possible. In doing this, a long rod is a great help and for that reason, if for no other, I am glad to see that the modern trend is towards marketing longer spinning rods.

The required modification in technique is merely, after casting, to keep the rod vertical, and as much line out of the water as possible until the bait enters the taking arc. Only then is the point of the rod dropped to water level. The bait will then sink to its effective fishing level very quickly and yet, during the period when a fish is most likely to take, the rod and line will be correctly aligned so as to obtain effective hooking.

So much for my thoughts on bait-fishing. I can understand that some people like or dislike it, as a form of fishing, in the sense that they enjoy, or do not enjoy, practising it themselves. What I cannot understand is the blind, unreasoning hostility to it one sometimes encounters. I am not a particularly enthusiastic bait-fisher myself, and seldom get the bait-rod out except in the early spring, but that is a matter of preference and not prejudice. I welcome sensible rules regulating its use because in certain circumstances (low-water conditions for example) the fly is so much to be preferred as less likely to disturb or foul-hook fish. In normal conditions, however, I do not believe that the bait-fisher is likely to do either of these things, or that (provided the prawn is banned) he enjoys some unfair or unsporting advantage over the fly-fisher which ought to be curbed. During, or immediately after, a big rise in water he may have a greater chance of a fish than someone fishing the fly, but that is fair enough, surely? At other times, except in the early spring when there are no restrictions on its use and no one seems to object to it, it does not, in my experience, confer any particular advantage in terms of fish caught, often the reverse in fact, and prejudice against it seems inexplicable.

Why, then, does spinning engender so much hostility? I suppose it is because it happens to be a tool suited for deliberate foul-hooking. On the other hand, the sunk fly can also be most skilfully employed by deliberate foul-hookers, but no one, as far as I am aware, is at all hostile to the sunk fly, as a method, or seeks to curtail its use in low-water conditions.

I find these inconsistencies particularly puzzling because I have fished, and still do, rivers where the fly-fisher and the bait-fisher coexist perfectly satisfactorily and happily; where the upstream Mepps or Toby is accepted as a perfectly legitimate and fair method of fishing, as indeed it is. Yet on another river, where there is hostility to the use of the bait, one is in danger of having one's integrity impugned if one makes so much as a square cast with a bait rod. This makes no sense to me at all, especially as, on that river, the bait may only be fished when the river is big and when the chances of foul-hooking are infinitesimal.

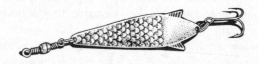

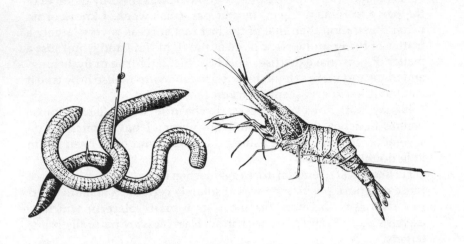

— 29 —

Prawning and Worming

Most of my knowledge of prawning and worming derives from a very old friend, now deceased. He was more dedicated than any other salmon fisher I have ever known, or am likely to know, and when he died all his fishing friends recognised that their lives would henceforth be the poorer.

If George had any interests other than fishing, he disguised them well. When he was present it was no use trying to have a general conversation. He would just lie in wait and, at the first opportunity, bring it round to his favourite subject.

He was not just a fly-only man. He maintained, and I believe he was right, that if one wishes to know a subject really well one has to study everything about it. All aspects of the sport were therefore as grist to his mill, and he became an artist at them all.

With the fly and the minnow, George had the distinction of killing more fish in a single day than any other man with whom I have had personal contact. And yet, when I was fishing with him on one occasion and sport was reasonably good, he was the only member of the party to remain 'clean' in that particular week. I know of no better illustration than that of the fact that success is very largely a matter of being in the right place at the right time and is not just a matter of personal expertise. This is particularly true of fly-fishing, and more and more salmon fishers are coming to realise how true it is. Only the experts seem reluctant to admit it.

It may not, however, necessarily be true when fishing those bonnes-bouches the prawn and the worm. I have watched, on several occasions, George fishing these baits and have been left in little doubt about that.

He liked best to employ them against fish he could actually see, or those of whose position he was absolutely certain. A shallow, narrow river was therefore the most appropriate place in which to exercise his skill, and potted fish in such a river were naturally prime targets.

His technique with both baits was the same – that of the clear-water wormer. Having selected his target he would cast the bait, virtually unweighted, several yards upstream so that the current would bring it down as close past the side of the fish as possible. He maintained that extreme accuracy in doing this was essential, especially with a potted fish, otherwise such a cabbage, living in a fishy world of its own, would not have its taste-buds stimulated sufficiently for it to respond.

Response could vary considerably, and in one of his letters he gave me a remarkable description of how he had watched a group of fish deal with a bunch of worms. For some days previously, sport had been good because there had been rain, and fish had been taking the worm with a will, the hooks invariably ending up in, or near, their stomachs. Then the river had fallen to a low level and, although some fish still seemed to be interested, it became impossible to hook them. At the head of one of his favourite worming pools there was a huge rock from which it was possible to see what was going on below, and George had stationed himself there in order to do so. He described to me how he had seen fish after fish stimulated to inspect the bait, pick it up by the tip of one of the worms, carry it for a few yards and then drop it. As far as he could tell, not a single fish had actually taken the bunch properly into its mouth during the whole period he was watching, and he thought that this was an amazing illustration of their extreme delicacy of touch.

I think he was right in assuming that it is the taste of these baits rather than their visual details which stimulates potted fishes' interest in them. This seems to be confirmed by the fact that they can be stimulated to take bits of prawn which bear no resemblance to any actual creature, and will ignore the artificial prawn which does. Moreover, although prawn fishers normally take great pains to mount their baits as naturally as possible, this obviously cannot be the decisive factor because, on at least one occasion to my knowledge, the prawn has produced sensational results when mounted, by mistake, back to front. Be that as it may, George was very particular about taste, and liked to use fresh prawns, salted, in preference to any others.

I never heard George say that he had seen fish become terrified of the prawn, as is commonly believed can happen sometimes, and it is now too late to ask him. He certainly believed that the prawn was a bait which should only be employed for a few casts and then discarded if the fish were not 'on' it.

If it does terrify fish sometimes, and cause them to take off for points east and west when they see it, I think it strange that its use is tolerated on some rivers, and on others is not merely tolerated but expressly permitted. On one such river, where I fish at some time in most years, I have the impression that fish apparently become so accustomed to being offered prawns that they will virtually ignore them, only the occasional one falling victim to them. Perhaps someone there gets a sensational bag at some time or other during the season, but if so I haven't heard of it.

If, in general, prawns when used persistently become no more effective than any other bait, why not ban them? If there is *any* danger of their terrifying fish, this surely is the obvious thing to do? But perhaps all these stories of fish being frightened by them, and practically jumping on to the bank to avoid them, are just a lot of old wives' tales. I have never once seen them do it, myself.

In fact, if I were to be asked, I would give it as my opinion that salmon were totally unafraid of anything *in the water*, other than otters and mink. Cautious, but nevertheless unafraid, as far as I have ever been able to see.

Movement *on the bank* is quite another matter. They are clearly more than just cautious about that.

You would think that if they were to become terrified of anything 'fishy' it would be of lampreys. But I have seen a couple of lampreys harassing a salmon, which could have moved off or disposed of them with a couple of quick bites whenever it liked, and the fish did no more than move away a foot or two at a time.

On the other hand fish will display caution to a marked degree sometimes. They will even drop back down a pool which is being fished with the fly, making a wide detour back to their lies in order to avoid being covered by it. If the fly can have that effect it seems quite possible that the prawn could produce a more violent reaction on occasion.

Personally I would prefer it if the prawn and the worm were to be banned on all the rivers I fish. This is primarily because, once they are permitted, recourse to these baits is invariably overdone. I am forced to admit, however, that there is knowledge to be gained from using them, and that this can be very helpful in aiding our understanding of the sport as a whole. I am therefore most grateful to George for helping me to acquire some of it because, almost certainly, it is knowledge I would never have acquired for myself.

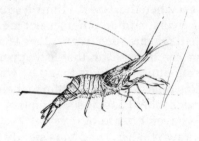

—— 30 ——

The End of the Season

With the arrival of September, which for years I have spent in fishing a spring river, my emotions always become confused. On the one hand it is a time for light-heartedness, for family fishing and relaxation, but, on the other, a time of great sadness because the end of the season is fast approaching like some terrible affliction.

The feeling of sadness can be held at bay for a while if sport is good, because this will occupy the mind to the exclusion of much else, so the portents are always anxiously scanned when the time for back-end fishing approaches. If the first frosts of winter have occurred early, followed by rain to bring the river up to a good level, the chances are that sport will be good. The fish population will then have come to life, so to speak, and begun to move up river slowly towards the redds, so takers will abound. If the river remains big enough, fresh fish, which were absent in August, will again put in an appearance although, alas, not in great numbers where I and my family fish. September can therefore be the ideal time for the young, or beginners. They can enjoy good sport without worry, because their inexperience and relative ineptitude will be unimportant in fishy terms, provided that they have been properly taught how to return to the water, unharmed, any gravid fish they may catch.

We have strict rules about this, in my party. Fresh fish may be kept but, of the others, only males. Of these, moreover, the ones which are not in good enough condition to eat, or are unsuitable for smoking, must also be returned. In other words we return most of the fish we catch in September, and considerable care is taken to ensure that everyone knows how to do this.

From time to time I hear opinions that most of the fish thus released will surely die, and that in consequence it is a useless exercise. I suspect that these are the views of people who have an ulterior motive, and would like to see back-end fishing banned on spring rivers. There seems to be no evidence to support their contention. I have been catching and releasing back-end salmon for many, many years and have always been perfectly satisfied that they survive, provided that the release is gone about in the proper manner.

One has to take time about it, though; it is no good just putting the fish back in the water and hoping for the best. It is essential to be at pains to find a nice comfortable spot, where there is enough flow but not too much, where the fish can be propped up with stones and, if necessary, left. Often this means trying several places before settling on the right one. When such a place has been found, the hold on the fish's tail should not be relinquished until there is no doubt that the fish will remain upright. If it tends to fall over to one side or the other when this grip is relaxed, tighten the grip again. Watch the dorsal fin. When this begins to operate so as automatically to keep the fish on an even keel, it is possible to start thinking about leaving it, but never leave it until certain that it will be all right.

Sometimes I have gone back a couple of hours later to find the fish still lying where I left it. Sometimes it has moved a yard or two of its own accord to a more comfortable place. Invariably it goes off like a rocket as soon as it sees me, leaving no doubt about its ability to look after itself again.

Some of these fish were out of the water for two or three minutes while the fly was extracted and the fish weighed, but I do all I can to keep this time to the minimum. For the former process I carry artery forceps and for the latter a special spring-balance which enables the fish to be weighed by the tail. If a net is carried, the fish is weighed in that.

These are mostly gravid fish but, as they clearly take no harm, their condition is immaterial to survival.

As I say, I have never felt the slightest misgivings about releasing fish successfully provided that it is done with the necessary care, but it was nevertheless heartening to read, the other day, an article in the International Atlantic Salmon Foundation's *Bulletin* confirming my feelings about it. The article described a three-year 'catch and release' programme, carried out in Icelandic waters, which proved beyond doubt that released fish do in fact survive, and that it is just a myth that they do not.

In this programme, fish were caught with rod and line, tagged and released. Many were subsequently re-caught. One, in fact, which seems to have had a sort of death-wish, was caught, tagged and released; caught a few days later and again released; and then, later, caught and released a third time. Another was caught again within twelve hours of being caught, tagged and released the first time, and was reported to be just as vigorous an adversary in its second battle as in its first.

The programme was carried out in the Grimsa, which is not a large river and has water which is generally clear and shallow. It was intensively fished for twelve hours a day throughout the seasons in question, so any dead fish would have been immediately observed. Only one was reported during the three years, and that one seemed to have sustained an injury to its gill structure, which may have accounted for its death.

The evidence provided by this programme is so conclusive that it should once and for all dispose of doubts about successfully releasing fish.

It gives me a chance to have one last tilt at the Lore, which always refers to the catching of trout but the *killing* of salmon. If it does this, as it probably does, because it reckons that salmon always fight their hearts out and that the level of lactic acid in their bodies inevitably builds up to the point where they cannot survive the struggle, then this is just one more example of the way it always latches on to old wives' tales and does its damnedest to perpetuate them. I am all for giving it one more poke in the eye, so let us start talking about catching salmon and stop talking about killing them!

181

If sport is bad in the back end it becomes for me a period when I have difficulty in fighting off the end-of-season blues. At other times, when sport is bad, I am accustomed to take time off, now and again, to listen to music. My car is fitted out for this, and the pleasure I derive from it has become part of the overall pleasure of being beside a salmon river. As with opera, in which the visual and the aural combine to maximise the effect, to watch the timeless river flowing by while listening to one of the great violin concertos, for example, is an experience calculated to move one to the very depths. This combination of sight and sound can be truly devastating, and make the tears of the soul pour out. The last few days of the season are not the time for it, however, because its effect is then altogether too painful. I used not to be like that. I used to be able to take as much masochistic pleasure in having my withers wrung then as at any other time, but not nowadays. With the passage of the years the prospect of making the last cast of the season has become something which engenders quite enough sadness of its own without deliberately adding to the emotional burden. So, in September, music is now *out*.

The emotional burden is in any case heavy enough in all conscience. The scents of autumn are in the air, the leaves are turning and the bloom on the heather has gone. There are goodbyes to old friends to be contemplated, tackle to be taken down and the motor car to be loaded. None of these are exactly joyful exercises.

When the time arrives for the hut door to be closed for the last time, symbolising the closure of another chapter, its dead sound is like a knell. Up to that moment the season has remained in the present, and one has still been part of it, involved in it. On the closing of the door it suddenly becomes the past, something more to be added to the days that are gone. There is next season to look forward to, of course, unless . . . ? There is always that question mark. No wonder the mood is sombre as one starts the journey home.

Appendix

Mr Wood's explanation of how he conceived the idea of greased-line fishing. Except for the last two sentences it appears to be no more than an explanation of how he came to devise his special hooking technique.

'I went to the head of the pool, which consisted of an eel-weir, and there found a number of salmon lying with their noses pushed right up against the sill. As luck had it, I happened to have with me a White Moth trout-fly; this I tied on the cast and sat on the plank-bridge over the weir. Then holding the gut in my hand, I dibbed the fly over them. After some minutes one of the salmon became curious enough to rise up to examine the fly, but at the last minute thought better of it; this I believe was due to its attention having been distracted by my feet, which were dangling over the plank, barely six feet away from the water. I changed my position, knelt on the bridge and let down the fly. This time the fish came more boldly at the fly and it was followed by others; but I had pricked several before I realised that, because I was kneeling directly over them, I was, in striking, pulling the hook straight out of their mouths. So I changed my tactics and, by letting go the cast at the right moment, succeeded in dropping the fly into the open mouth of the next fish that came up to it. I then picked up my rod, ran off the bridge, and made all haste downstream. All this time the line and cast were slack and floating down; yet when I tightened on the fish I found that it had hooked itself. By the use of this trick I landed six fish, lost others and pricked more than I care to say, all in a few hours. After that experience, I discovered myself fishing on the surface or as near to it as I was able. The final advance came when I started using a greased line to assist in keeping the fly in the right position . . .'

INDEX

Index

Index

189